∽✌

Father, Forgive Me, for I Am Frustrated

∽✌

Father, Forgive Me, for I Am Frustrated

*Growing in Faith When You
Don't Find It Easy Being Catholic*

MITCH PACWA, S.J.

CHARIS
Servant Publications
Ann Arbor, Michigan

Charis Books is an imprint of Servant Publications especially designed to serve Roman Catholics.

Although the stories in this book are true, some of the names of the individuals involved have been changed to protect their privacy.

Published by Servant Publications
P.O. Box 8617
Ann Arbor, Michigan 48107

96 97 98 99 00 10 9 8 7 6 5 4 3 2 1

Printed in the United States of America
ISBN 0-89283-840-X

LIBRARY OF CONGRESS CATALOGING-IN-PUBLICATION DATA

Pacwa, Mitch
    Father, forgive me, for I am frustrated : growing in your faith even when it isn't easy being Catholic / Mitch Pacwa.
        p. cm.
    Includes bibliographical references.
    ISBN 0-89283-840-X
    1. Spiritual formation—Catholic Church. 2. Spiritual life—Catholic Church. 3. Catholic Church—Doctrines. 4. Catholic Church—Membership. I. Title
BX2350.2.P258   1996
282'.73—dc21   96-40845
                                                                    CIP

Contents

DEDICATION

To my cousin, Missy Draus, cruelly murdered just before her seventeenth birthday. In our relationship after her father's death, she gave me a little glimpse into the reasons that dads have such a special love for their little girls. May her wonderful mother, Nancy, and two brothers, Joey and Matt, find comfort. May the Eternal Light shine upon Missy and grant her rest.

ONE

A Confession
of Frustrations

It has been a typical Sunday Mass in any one of thousands of typical Catholic parishes across the country. Dismissed with the usual exhortation to "go in peace," the congregation begins filing out. Unfortunately, however, many of these parishioners are going away filled not with the peace of Christ but with a sense of deep frustration over their experience of life in the Church. "Bless me, Father, I'm frustrated," is their common confession.

Larry and Loretta, a retired couple, move slowly out of the pew that they occupied every Sunday for years with their eight children. Those children are all grown up now, but only two are still practicing Catholics. Cults, agnosticism, and the pursuit of riches lured the other six away.

Bitter thoughts keep hounding the couple. *All those years we scrimped and saved to send our kids to Catholic schools— twelve years' worth for each one—and for what? What else could we have done? Why didn't our kids persevere in their faith?*

Paul and Esther are struggling with similar regrets about their daughter Linda. She and her family might well be attending Sunday Mass with them were it not for the lie she heard years ago in religion class at her Catholic school: "If you truly love a boy, it may be morally acceptable to have sexual intercourse before marriage. God is love."

Paul and Esther were anguished witnesses to the tragic sequence of events. Their daughter got pregnant (the same summer that the religious sister who had taught this nonsense left her order), got married, had two more children, and was abandoned by her husband at age twenty. Eventually Linda remarried and became a committed evangelical Christian like her husband. All the children attended their church's school and received the Christian moral training Linda had missed; today one son is a missionary to Catholics in Poland and another plays in a Christian rock band. But Linda herself is still bitter about her Catholic upbringing—and her parents feel let down and angry at the Church.

A few pews over, **Tim** is kneeling in prayer, apologizing to the Lord for having been so distracted during the liturgy. He just doesn't know how to react to yesterday's phone call from his daughter Jennifer. "Dad, the pastor refuses to perform a big church wedding for John and me," she told him angrily. "He says we have to stop living together first. Oh, he's willing to do a small private ceremony. But I want the big wedding I've always dreamed of!"

Tim is secretly relieved (he didn't think a big wedding

was appropriate either) and embarrassed that he hadn't known how to discuss the matter with Jennifer. He is also worried that this disappointment will turn Jennifer and John against the Church forever. *And just when they were showing such genuine interest, too. Lord, please don't let this drive them away.*

Across the aisle from Tim, **Sarah,** a single woman in her twenties, flounces out a side door to avoid having to greet the pastor. Not only does she find his homilies dull and irrelevant, but she is dissatisfied with his lack of spiritual leadership. Her parish is without life, she feels—no concern for the poor or for preaching the gospel, no Bible study or other help for growing spiritually, no sense of community. Two years ago Sarah experienced a deep renewal of her faith at a charismatic prayer meeting she still attends in another parish. *Why doesn't our pastor encourage something like that here?* she wonders in exasperation.

Chuck makes a decision as he gathers up his belongings from the pew where he has been sitting: next Sunday he will go to Mass at another parish, where things are done in the good old way—where the priest says Mass in Latin with his back to the people. "Enough is enough," Chuck mutters. He is still uncomfortable with the sign of peace, and he hardly goes to confession any more for fear of having to talk face to face with the confessor. Whether Vatican II was good or bad for the Church, Chuck isn't sure; he feels uninformed and knows only that he is uneasy about much of what is said to be "in the spirit of Vatican II."

Donna is uneasy too, which is why she is racing up the aisle after the pastor. Positioning herself at his elbow, she waits for him to finish greeting people. She simply must talk to him about what happened at the diocesan day of instruction for catechists that she has just attended.

Donna found the beginning of the meeting unsettling, when the diocesan head of religious education explained that Native Americans used burning sweetgrass as a form of blessing, much as Catholics use holy water. "It would be a nice idea to open our meeting with smoke offered to the spirits of the four directions," the leader proposed.

"None of us are Indians," one of the catechists protested. "We're Polish and Italian. Why don't we bless ourselves with holy water and the sign of the cross?" But the smoke ceremony won out. "It's more meaningful," the leader decided.

What in the world is going on in the Church? Donna wonders. Not that this is the first strange practice to have caught her attention. Workshops on witchcraft, the inner goddess, Celtic paganism, and the enneagram—Donna has seen all of these offered in parishes and religious education congresses and on Catholic college campuses. *But what can I do?* Donna keeps asking herself. *I'm just an ordinary person.*

Last one out of church is **Sister Stella,** a seventy-something nun who is experiencing great pain and sadness as she watches her congregation die before her eyes. In the 1950s her community numbered seven hundred sisters, with fifty young women entering each year to work at fifty-two elementary schools, six high schools, a college, two hospitals, and a retreat house. All that changed in the 1960s, when Sister Stella's congregation responded to Vatican II's call to renewal by experimenting with new liberties and lifestyles. Secular clothes quickly replaced the modified habit; house "coordinators" replaced superiors; private prayer replaced communal prayer. Sisters began taking on more "meaningful" work outside the community apostolates. Some also took on drinking, dating, and smoking—all tolerated as part of a process of growth and discernment of vocations.

Sister Stella and other older sisters objected, and the situation became so tense that the congregation split in two. The larger group of nuns were dispensed from their vows, and now follows a more secular way of life. Sister Stella belongs to the smaller, more traditional group, which now numbers about twenty-five nuns, half of them over eighty years old. Sister Stella feels betrayed by the former leaders of her community and grieved by the great scandal of her order's disruption.

WHY SO FRUSTRATED?

The above parish is mythical, but the stories are true—a representative sampling of the experiences of many Catholics in real-life parishes today. The reasons for their frustrations are as varied as the types of Catholics who are frustrated.

Many ordinary Catholics feel confused and even ignorant about their faith. Shaken by the changes that have taken place in the Church in the past thirty years, they wonder which beliefs still hold true. Catholics do not eat fish on Fridays anymore. Do they still believe in purgatory?

Does it even matter if you believe in purgatory or anything else, so long as you love everybody? What is the use of having an active church life? Doesn't everyone go to heaven anyway?

Many Catholics also admit to frustration over Church requirements and teaching. Birth control is one hot issue; so is remarriage, especially for Catholics who are divorced and feel punished by the Church's position. Chafing under these or other Church regulations that they don't understand, many men and women often reach the conclusion that "it's just too hard being Catholic."

Catholic parents struggle with the daunting challenge of passing on the faith in twentieth-century America. How can they get their children interested and involved? Why isn't there a parish school? (Or why isn't the existing parish school more effective? Or why is the waiting list so impossibly long?) Some parents resent having to participate in the parish programs that prepare their children for the sacraments; other parents fault the parish for not involving them enough.

Interview any representative group of typical Catholics in the pew, and you will discover quite a variety of frustrations. "I don't get anything out of Mass." "I miss the Marian processions and Sunday afternoon vespers and other devotions we used to have." "The parish seems dead." "We're always getting asked for money. And furthermore, I don't agree with how the money is used." "The pastor and most of the parish leaders really turn me off." "There are too many women involved in parish leadership." "There aren't enough women involved."

Catholics whose faith has been enkindled or mobilized through participation in renewal movements may be especially frustrated when they fail to find in their parishes what they have found elsewhere: vibrant and participative liturgies, or a sense of community, or a commitment to evangelism or prayer or social justice issues. Additional frustrations arise when the parish and the pastor are not receptive to such movements, or when the various groups within a parish compete instead of working together.

Finally, some Catholics are frustrated because they do not think the Church is moving (or not moving quickly enough) in the direction they desire. At one extreme are those who not only insist that the Church should return to what it was before Vatican II, but who mistrust every pope since Pius XII. At the other extreme are those whose agenda includes women's ordination, inclusive language that eliminates all masculine references to God, and a loosening of sexual morality.[1]

DEAD END APPROACHES

Life is hard and full of frustrating problems; that is the nature of life, even of life in the Church. The question, however, is not how to get rid of all problems (an impossible ideal), but rather how to deal with the problems we encounter. For some people, frustration works as a negative, destructive force. Others have learned how to put their frustration to work as a spur to positive action.

Because I am in contact with Catholics around the

world, many of them frustrated with life in their parishes or dioceses, I see quite a variety of positive and negative approaches to problems in the Church.

"I give up." This is the response of someone who has given in to discouragement and hopelessness, sometimes after making an attempt to change a particular situation. A typical conversation with such a person might begin with my asking, "What have you already done? Have you spoken to the people involved or, if necessary, to the pastor or bishop?"

"Yes, I have, but nothing ever happened."

"Have you tried getting on the parish council or becoming a catechist or other type of volunteer?"

"Yes, I've tried all that."

"Are you praying about the situation?"

"Yes but with no results. Everything I attempt fails. I quit."

The saddest situation is when Catholics claim to believe in Christ, his teachings, and his Church but despair of any renewal or change. "The liberals have too much control in the diocesan liturgy commission." "My pastor thinks I'm a nut and a troublemaker." "I feel spiritually undernourished in the Church." "My situation is hopeless."

Of course, the situation would be hopeless if the Church were merely a human enterprise. But it is not. The Church of Christ is a community established and sustained by God Almighty. The Father's power and grace, salvation by Jesus Christ, and the abiding of the Holy Spirit form the basis for hope of Catholic renewal.

Catholics who feel defeated must cling to this truth and ask God for an infusion of hope, or they may give up completely on what seems an impossible battle and lapse into apathy and indifference. They may even drift quietly out of the Church.

Hopelessness about problems can also express itself as a fixation with the end of the world, or at least a major chastisement. For some Catholics, this preoccupation emerges out of a despair over whether God can act in the present world anymore. They have no hope that God can use them for ministry or the conversion of sinners. They assume that society cannot be brought back to good morals and decency, so they consult various visionaries and mystics and wait for the end.

What these Catholics forget is that God alone knows the day and hour of Christ's return and is completely in charge. The Christian on earth is in sales, God is management. God will manage the end times. The Christian's task is to be holy and good, announce the gospel to as many people as possible, and persevere in the good deeds God requires.

"I'll do it my way." Another unhealthy response to difficulties comes from Catholics who seek to resolve their frustrations by ignoring or defying Church teaching and practice. "Cafeteria Catholics" fall into this category—those who pick and choose from among the Church's doctrines, adhering only to those which appeal to them as the most beautiful or reasonable or politically correct.

In the United States this rejection of Church teaching has been accelerated by the controversy over birth control.

As Ann Roach Muggeridge explains in her book, *The Desolate City: Revolution in the Catholic Church*,[2] the crisis about sexual morals in response to Pope Paul VI's encyclical *Humanae Vitae* has galvanized a revolution within the Catholic Church, much as the Boston Tea Party, the storming of the Bastille, and the Alamo galvanized revolutions in the American colonies, France, and Texas. As the arguments and debates spread from sexual morals to other areas of doctrine, many Catholics have been left with the impression that everything is up for question.

Especially confusing is the fact that many of the people who are denying Church doctrine are the priests, religious, and lay Catholic leaders who are expected to promote it.[3] Some justify this as a "modern" strategy to keep people within the Church by adapting Catholic morals and doctrine to society's trends and beliefs.

Many Catholics who are frustrated or confused by some Church teaching or practice simply disobey it quietly. Others go public, working for change in the Church by using a civil disobedience model borrowed from the protest movements or from community organizing. Therefore, when Rome did not allow the laity to receive Communion in the hand, the practice was simply done without permission as a way to force the issue. The use of girl altar servers was prohibited but some parishes used them anyway until the Vatican accepted it.

As a result of such experiences, some advocates of change feel they will get nowhere with the official Church unless they are disobedient to those norms they disagree with. They feel prophetic in stating their positions and acting on them. When their personal beliefs contradict papal statements, they still consider themselves "good Catholics," a sort of loyal opposition party.[4]

Nor is such disobedience limited to those frustrated Church members who have liberal views. Some Catholics who claim to be orthodox use their conservatism as a screen for denying Church teaching. Their denials are often as unwitting and well-intentioned as those of many liberals, but the unraveling of the fabric of the faith is just as real.

Some of these Catholics look primarily to visionaries and locutionists for direction on everything from how to reform the Church to how to cast their ballot in U.S. elections. A few of them claim that Pope Paul VI was kidnapped and replaced by an impostor. Denying that a valid pope has reigned since then, they no longer accept papal teaching, and they see themselves as victims of plots and conspiracies orchestrated by Vatican liberals.

Some of the most conservative Catholics, completely fed up with the present state of the Church, commit the sin of schism. They join the followers of Archbishop Lefebvre, for instance, or the offshoots of his schism. They set up chapels around the United States to have the Tridentine Mass, often celebrated by priests ordained by schismatic bishops.

Many times these arch-conservatives offer valid criticisms of the destructive influence of those Catholics who have lost their faith and yet remain within the Church to damage the faith of others. However, they forget our blessed Lord's parables, which teach that Satan will sow weeds among the wheat (Mt 13:24-31, 36-43) and the dragnet will bring in good fish and bad (Mt 13:47-59). They have given up hope that the present situation can be resolved, and so they separate themselves from the Church which Christ established.

A BETTER WAY

Fortunately, I am in contact not only with frustrated Catholics who see no solution to their problems—or none that is in line with Church teaching—but also with frustrated Catholics who are taking some positive steps. Their experience offers hope for all of us who are dissatisfied by some aspect of life in the Church. It indicates that there is a constructive way to deal with the nagging frustrations that block our spiritual lives.

Of course, no book can cover every problem and offer solutions for the wide variety of challenges that Catholics of all types experience. But this book will present an approach that any Catholic can use to overcome frustration and foster personal and corporate spiritual growth. Without proposing specific solutions, it will suggest a common strategy that can make a difference in our experience of life in the Church. This approach comprises six basic elements that we will examine more closely in the following chapters.

Goals. Setting goals is an important first step in moving out of frustration and toward positive change in our lives as Catholics. Without goals we are aimless, merely reacting to crises or other people's actions. Without the right goals, we will move in the wrong direction and only contribute to the current confusion in the Church. Any strategy for personal change or for specific improvements must be grounded in the larger context of Christ's goals for our lives and for the Church.

Repentance. People who are frustrated with their experience of life have a tendency to pin the blame on others. We must resist this tendency and begin our work for change by confessing our own sins, not other people's. Making a fresh start requires that we take responsibility for the actions and attitudes that have blocked our growth. Persevering in our efforts and in Christ's goals requires ongoing repentance.

Prayer. No frustrated Catholic can afford to neglect prayer and meditation. Prayer is a channel of grace through which God changes things. God can change us by relieving our frustrations and by making us more Christlike instruments for renewal in the Church. He can change the situations that we find difficult—either through direct intervention or through some insight or action that he inspires.

Education. How can we act intelligently to deal with our feelings of frustration and to counter abuses if we do not have a good grasp of our faith? Perhaps some of our frustrations would not be problems if we understood them better. Perhaps we would take wiser, more confident action if we were more solidly grounded in our faith. Scripture, Church documents and doctrinal works, histories, lives of the saints—the Church offers us a wealth of wisdom that will enrich our lives and others', if only we tap into it.

Action. Prepared through repentance, prayer, and study, we are ready to take practical steps to change the situations that frustrate us. Discernment will help us see and choose which doors of opportunity to walk through; creativity will expand our notions of how and where we might work for change. Here, the example of other Catholics who have acted and achieved improvement is especially important: it can inspire us to address our own specific problems with great confidence in the Lord.

Endurance. Sometimes change in our local situation comes slowly. Some things may change only a little, or not at all. Great efforts may yield only puny results. Setbacks and failures will certainly come to each of us, and when they do we can learn to grow in wisdom through them. Our Lord may be allowing these frustrations for our good—perhaps so that we will become patient and enduring. And in every suffering Jesus is with us, conforming us to his image as he helps us carry our cross.

SO PROBLEMS ARE GOOD FOR ME?

Some people respond to difficulties as opportunities rather than stumbling blocks, as exciting challenges rather than obstacles. This is most strikingly true of the saints, who turned their frustrations and difficulties to the greatest advantage of all.

Just as apparent flaws in a diamond can become the opportunity for the unique cut that increases its value, so do problems provide the means through which ordinary Catholics rise above the ordinary and become saints. Ever notice how many saints throughout history grew in holiness by working to renew the Church at some of its lowest ebbs?

How many saints rose up during the Protestant Reformation! Famous for church corruption and religious revolt, this period marked the first of three times that vocations decreased in the history of the Church. Nonetheless, God brought forth great saints like John of God, Charles Borromeo, Pope Pius V. Many arose as founders of religious orders—among them, Ignatius of Loyola, Jerome Emiliani, and Anthony Zaccaria—or reformers of orders, like Teresa of Avila and John of the Cross.

Five million European Christians left the Church during this tumultuous period. And yet, over thirty million people became Catholics in the Spanish colonies, and the Church spread to Africa and Asia. Jesuit missionaries evangelized new countries (St. Francis Xavier baptized more people than anyone else in history), re-evangelized Europe (like St. Peter Canisius), and were martyred for the faith (like the missionary saints Paul Miki and John de Britto, and St. Andrew Bobola in Europe). Two other well-known saints, Bishop John Fisher and Thomas More, were martyred during this period. Indeed, a multitude of saints sprang up in this troubled time.

The second period of decline in vocations took place during the French Revolution. The Society of Jesus was suppressed everywhere except in the Russian Empire; other religious orders were expelled from France and Spain before the Revolution. During the Revolution, churches were desecrated, priests and nuns martyred, and the pope imprisoned.

But this was only a temporary setback for the Church, because hundreds of new orders were founded in the aftermath. These communities—the reconstituted Jesuits, the Society of the Divine Word, the Society of Mary, and so many others—journeyed to the newly explored continents to engage in the most successful period of conversion in history. The groups of martyrs of Korea, Vietnam, and elsewhere, plus individuals like St. Peter Chanel, were the seeds that blossomed into new churches that are still growing.

The present time, the revolutionary nature of which may be based on the issue of sexuality, is only the third period of decline in religious vocations in the Church. Will this era, like the two that preceded it, also be a period when many men and women respond to the call to holiness? It can be, if those who have faith in Christ Jesus transform the problems into opportunities for the creative, energetic actions that characterized the best and most grace-filled responses to previous crises.

Problems challenged the saints of the past to become holy. The same is true today. Modern Church problems are not overwhelming catastrophes but fantastic challenges for each Catholic to grow in holiness. Active pursuit of holiness is like the pressure on coal before it turns into diamonds. God can effect wonderful transformations with life's pressures and the heat of his loving grace!

The question is: Will we become saints by cooperating with Christ in facing our problems and renewing the

Church? Or will we whine so much that we become a problem for someone else who is trying to become a saint?

HOPE FOR THE FRUSTRATED

Frankly, I am a frustrated Catholic too. The modern confusion causes me pain. Liturgical abuses, denials of the faith by Catholics, and distortions of Catholic doctrine and morals by theologians cause me much distress. Catholics who spend more time reading condemned books like Maria Valtorta's *The Poem of the Man-God* than the Gospels cause me grief. Enthusiastic crowds who flock to certain visionaries without discerning their errors of faith distress me. Any Catholic who is not actively engaged in the Church's mission of winning the whole world to Jesus Christ, his true gospel, and the Church he established makes me sad.

However, I refuse to let these problems overwhelm me. I believe that Christ's cross is more powerful than any sin, lack of faith, spiritual crisis, or frustrating situation. Our Lord is infinitely more concerned with the conversion of hearts and minds than I ever can be, since he loves every person infinitely. He cares about my frustrations and stands ready to help me deal with them. Because of all this, I have hope that my efforts can have real effect—both in changing the specific situations I find difficult and in contributing to the renewal of the Church.

With confidence in Christ, I am willing to be at his disposal to serve him and his Church in any way I can. I trust that he is stirring up a large number of other hearts to do the same.

TWO

≈

What Do You Want?

As a boy I tried to fix old radios, clocks, and watches. I took them apart, looked for the problem, and reassembled them. None of them ever worked because I had no plans or directions to consult, and I was clueless about how the repaired product was supposed to look. Without the maker's goal in mind, I ended up with leftover parts and wires and forever useless appliances.

The Church is far more complex than any appliance, of course, but a similar principle applies for frustrated Catholics who want to take action. That is, before trying to fix any of the problems we encounter in our life in the Church, we need to know the mind of its Founder. It is not enough to set our own specific personal goals. The goals must be true and right; they must fit into the larger context of Christ's goals. Successful change and renewal occurs only when Catholics follow the Manufacturer's plan.

Fortunately, the One who created human beings and

founded the Church has revealed his goals and purposes for us through Christ. In Scripture and the teaching of the Church, we find objective norms for discerning whether our human plans and ideas conform to the Creator's. Here is where we must begin if we want to improve our experience of life within the Church.

One approach to reflect on God's goals is to examine the goals that flow from our redemption through Jesus Christ. The biblical images of Jesus Christ as Priest, Prophet, and King shed light on various aspects of salvation and on the specific goals they entail.

CHRIST OUR PRIEST REDEEMER

Jesus Christ is the one true high priest who saves the world once and for all by offering himself as a sacrifice for the remission of sin. His priesthood lasts for all eternity, making possible the salvation of all who draw near to God through him (Heb 7:23-25). His self-offering is limitless in its power to forgive all people from every sin; it can touch sinners in all times and in every place. Jesus our Lord claims this reconciliation as the purpose for which he came: "The Son of Man came not to be served but to serve and offer his life as a ransom for many" (Mk 10:45). His purpose of reconciling sinners to God calls each of us to two particular means.

First, we make an act of faith in Christ and his power to save. We believe that Christ's death and resurrection really have the power to forgive our offenses against the infinite, eternal, and all-good God. The faith that trusts Christ to forgive our sins leads us to confess these sins and to renounce further sinning. Faith accepts that Christ has power to transform any lingering desires to sin or sinful distortions. Jesus our Lord wants to pour out the indispensable grace that transforms our lives and restores us to the image and likeness of God.

Second, we commit ourselves to Christ and follow him as he asks. This necessarily entails picking up the cross with Jesus and following him—something we could never do if he had not won for us the grace to die to ourselves. But Christ has experienced the fullness of death and grants us the grace of dying to all our sins so that we can rise to holiness, love, justice, and all other virtue. Dying to ourselves and carrying our cross may seem like gloomy goals at first, but in doing so, repentant sinners discover an interior peace that lightens their struggles against sin.

CHRIST AS PROPHET

As a prophet, Jesus Christ came to teach about God's relationship to the world and its people. Believing and living these teachings is an important goal for all Christians.

St. John's Gospel identifies Jesus as the Word of God—which the Fathers of the Church understood as being the perfect and infinite self-knowledge of the Father, personified in Jesus. In fact, the only way to know the Father is through the Word: "No one can come to the Father except through me," Jesus said (Jn 14:6). Christ gives us access to the Father in the Holy Spirit so that we can share in the divine nature.

At the same time, Christ fully reveals what it means to be human, for he is the perfect man who restores the divine image and likeness which had been disfigured by sin. To be fully human is a high calling: it means being perfect as our heavenly Father is perfect (Mt 5:48), compassionate as our Father is compassionate (Lk 6:36), holy as God is holy (Lv 19:2; 1 Pt 1:16).

Teaching with the authority to set moral goals for the whole human race, Jesus deepened the meaning of the first and second laws of the Old Testament: Love God with whole heart, soul, and mind; and love your neighbor as yourself (Mk 12:30-31; Lv 19:18). He made his own love for his followers the norm for loving one another (Jn 13:34; 15:12). Not only are murder and adultery forbidden, but so are the anger and lust within the heart. Instead, Christ Jesus asks for prayer, fasting, and almsgiving that come from the heart and are done for God alone (Mt 6:1-18). Trust in God must be total, with no admixture of trust in riches or one's own power (Mt 6:19-21, 25-34).

Christ, the great prophet and the perfect man, reveals the height of love of God and neighbor, and the holiness and virtue of which every person is capable by divine grace. Holding before us the goal of becoming fully human, Christ gives us the grace to attain it.

CHRIST THE KING

Jesus Christ is a king who exercises divine power in the world he created. His role as king fulfills the Old Testament messianic prophecies, which promised David a descendant who would rule on his throne for all eternity (see 2 Sm 7:13; Ps 89:19-37; 132:11-12). From the New Testament we learn that Christ the King will rule human hearts and give them the power to follow his prophetic teachings, and he will come to judge the living and the dead.

Christ's powerful role as king presents us with critical choices. Will we choose goals that coincide with his, or will we fight against him? Will we make it a life goal to reject sinful behavior and join the kingdom of God that Jesus brings to earth? Will we accept Jesus Christ as our king, and allow him to direct our life through his teaching and the personal vocation he gives us?

Of course, Christ the King wants everyone to seek the kingdom of God wholeheartedly, as if for the best pearl or a hidden treasure (Mt 13:44-45), for at the end of our lives he will judge each of us as saved or condemned according to our deeds. The redeemed he will transform to become as he is; the evil he will consign to eternal punishment.

Acknowledging Christ as our king implies two other key goals for every Catholic.

Preach Christ to the whole world. That Jesus himself considered this an important goal is evident from the fact that he opened his public ministry with the announcement,

"Repent, for the kingdom of God is at hand!" (Mt 4:17; Mk 1:15). The first time he sent out his disciples on a mission, he told them to preach the exact same message (Mt 10:7; Lk 9:2; 10:9). Not only that but, "go forth and make disciples of all nations" was Jesus' parting directive to the disciples (see Mt 28:18-20).

Unfortunately, a lot of Catholics today do not put much value on preaching the gospel to all people. Once some students invited me to a discussion group in a dormitory, along with a religious brother from campus ministry. When the students asked what I saw as the goal of a Jesuit university, I responded that we would want every student to become a good Catholic. This means conversion to Jesus Christ, baptism and the other sacraments, and the living of a moral life. The brother from campus ministry was dumbfounded. His mouth dropped and he sputtered as he asked, "Are you serious?"

"Of course!" I answered enthusiastically. "This is not a goal I chose on my own; Christ gave this goal to his Church. My role is to get with his program." In fact, some of my happiest moments as a professor include the baptism of some students and hearing confessions after having given my classes a test on the Ten Commandments. (And if they think *my* tests are hard, wait until they take God's.)

God "wishes all men to be saved and come to the knowledge of the truth" (1 Tm 2:4). God sent his Son, the Word made flesh, anointed by the Spirit to preach the gospel to the poor; to heal the contrite in heart (Is 61:1; Lk 4:18); to be a bodily and spiritual medicine.[5] Perhaps to the surprise of the religious brother above, Vatican II expresses the desire to shed Christ's radiance, which brightens the Church, on all men by proclaiming the gospel to every creature (Mk 16:15). Truly, the Church's goal is to bring all humanity with all its riches back to Christ its head in the unity of the Holy Spirit.[6]

Preaching the gospel includes striving for the unity of the Church that Christ decreed and prayed for. Christ's goal is unity (Eph 4). He founded one Church on the rock of Peter (Mt 16:18), and he prayed that the Church would be one (Jn 17:20-23). Therefore the Church never ceases to pray, hope, and work that the brothers and sisters who are separated into other churches may become one with the Catholic Church.[7]

This is not some out-of-date desire of an imperialistic past. Vatican II proclaims universal evangelization as the Church's central goal and intention: that God's kingdom may come and that the salvation of the whole human race may come to pass.[8] Each committed Catholic will therefore make it a personal goal to become God's instrument for proclamation of the gospel of Christ. This obligation is imposed on every disciple, according to the ability and opportunities of each.[9] With St. Paul the whole Church says, "Woe to me if I do not preach the gospel" (1 Cor 9:16).

Of course, our evangelization of the world is possible only by accepting the Holy Spirit. He is the active force who empowers any authentic proclamation of the gospel and reform within the Church.

Praise and glorify God. Every member of God's kingdom, and indeed of the whole human race, is created to give praise and glory to God, our great King, in word and deed. Praise expresses thanksgiving for all the good that God our Lord has given and done in the world. It admires the beauty and majesty of nature as a reflection of God's own greatness. It recognizes the powerful salvation won by Christ's death and resurrection and hopes for deliverance from danger and forgiveness of sin. Praise acknowledges the divine majesty, goodness, and glory of God simply because God is worthy of all honor and thanksgiving. For the greater glory of God were we created.

Praise is expressed both in our explicit worship and in our lives and actions. Praise is given when people are "filled with the fruit of righteousness which comes through Jesus Christ for the glory and praise of God" (Phil 1:11). People give praise to God through their labor to improve life, when they act on God's mandate to subject the world and its creatures and to govern it with justice and holiness. As Vatican II points out, their labor unfolds the Creator's work and contributes to the unfolding of God's plan in history.[10]

Therefore, every decision to be moral and holy in ordinary life is an act of praise to the Lord who is good. All labor to improve the world, serve others, and fulfill duties constitutes praise of the Creator of the world.

Finally, the act of praising God transforms every human effort. Praise is always appropriate and beneficial—not only when things have gone successfully but also when problems, challenges, and even disasters occur. Praising God during the hard times transforms us into more effective instruments in God's hands. "Rejoice in the Lord always, again I say, rejoice!" (Phil 4:4)—here is yet another of God's goals for the Christian life.

Knowing Christ's goals for his Church and for the whole human race is vital and challenging. But intellectual knowledge alone will not motivate us to apply them. For that we must also stir up desire and commitment. One effective way to mobilize this head knowledge and stir up desire is to meditate on why Christ gives us these goals: to obtain heaven and avoid hell.

NEEDED: A HEALTHY FEAR OF HELL

Who is afraid of hell today? Too few people even think about it, let alone fear it. Many people indulge in sinful behaviors without any thought of paying a price. This short-sighted view calls for a strong dose of reality therapy in actions and consequences. For example, speeding past a police car will lead to a ticket. Having sexual relations with multiple partners increases the risks of contracting sexually transmitted diseases. Committing serious sins precludes a person's entry into the kingdom of heaven.

Scripture is very clear on this point. "The works of the flesh are apparent," says the apostle Paul. "They are fornication, impurity, sensuality, idolatry, magic, hostility, rivalry, jealousy, rage, selfishness, dissensions, factions, envy, drunkenness, orgies, and things such as these. I tell you as I told you before: those who do such things will not inherit the kingdom of God" (Gal 5:19-21; see also 1 Cor 6:9-10;

Eph 5:5; Rv 21:27; 22:15). And Jesus Christ our Lord expresses an even more rigorous standard in the Sermon on the Mount (see Mt 5:21-48). Insistently and repeatedly, Jesus warns about the eternal punishment in store for those who commit serious sin. His message is clear: Live in such a way as to avoid hell!

This message is not often heard from the pulpit today, but the Church's greatest preachers and spiritual directors have always recognized its importance and effectiveness. For example, the consequence of sin is a central theme of St. Ignatius of Loyola's *Spiritual Exercises*, a classic manual for directing retreats, which has been a powerful means of conversion for four hundred years. St. Ignatius begins the first week of the *Exercises* by inviting retreatants to meditate on their sins, and he ends it by proposing that they imagine and meditate on hell. Being deeply convinced that hell is not the place to be can be powerful motivation to keep away from sin.

Is fear of hell a less noble motive than the love of heaven? Perhaps a better question to ask is: Does it work?

Stop and think about the way people are motivated to change their lives in other areas. The pain of hangovers did more to keep me from excess drinking than did dad's descriptions of a happy, healthy liver. Recent movements toward a new chastity are prompted more by a fear of sexually transmitted diseases than by a love of purity.

And do people stop smoking just because it is more noble not to smoke? My mother stopped after she found out she had cancer. Other friends stopped when they knew relatives who had cancer or emphysema. People who can no longer taste their food want to savor flavors again.

Young smokers who cannot keep up with a middle-aged man like me while climbing the stairs or walking in canyons decide they need to change their habits. Smokers tired of being hassled by non-smoking prohibitions eventually stop. In other words, smokers stop when they are sufficiently put off by the bad effects of smoking.

People quit smoking and begin healthy eating patterns because they fear sickness or a painful death. Similarly, the fear of going to hell often prevents me from committing sins. Meditating on the reality of hell is all the motivation we need to change our living habits to conform with the way of life God has set for us.

"But I do not want to believe in a God who would punish people and make them afraid," some people object. "I believe in a *loving* God." Of course God our Lord is a loving God. But he is not ignorant of the evil in the world and in human hearts. Can you imagine a heavenly banquet where Hitler sits next to Mother Teresa to justify his murder of the Jews? I don't think so! If we ignore warnings to humanity about the dangers of damnation, then we reject the God that Jesus Christ reveals to us through the gospels.

SET YOUR HEART ON HEAVEN

We all need positive goals to shoot for, not just dangers to avoid. In the Christian life fear of what is bad, namely hell, should yield more and more to love for the good, namely heaven. Pope St. Gregory the Great comments on this dynamic:

...the holy Church of the elect sets out along the path of simplicity and righteousness in fear, but finishes in love. For it is the Church's task to turn completely away from evil; once she has begun by love of God, she rejects sin. If she still does good only out of fear, then inwardly she has not withdrawn from evil; for she commits sin by desiring to sin, if only she could sin without punishment.[11]

Christ Jesus our Lord set before us the goal of eternal life with God in heaven as the purpose of life to which all moral and charitable acts are directed. This call is the basis of the Christian virtue of hope, which redirects the heart from an attitude of fear to one of love. Since Christ invites all his disciples to enter his eternal joys, how important it is to set our hearts on heaven!

Meditating on heaven, like meditating on hell, can renew our resolve to pursue the right goals. Following Jesus is easier if the desire for heaven is established deep within our heart, mind, and imagination. So consider for a moment: What comes to mind when you think of heaven?

My earliest image of heaven was of a magnificent (in those days we said "boss") HO electric train set. Tunnels, mountains, switches, and smoking steam engines were all mine to set up, rearrange, and play with, without Mom calling me to wash up and eat. This little boy's idea of delight was based on dreams of his favorite toys. Adults, too, tend to think of heaven as an extension of what they love best. For example, St. Bridget of Ireland expressed a rather surprising view of heaven in a poem:

I would like a great lake of beer for the King of Kings.
I would like to be watching heaven's family
drinking it through all eternity.[12]

Naturally, our thinking about heaven should begin with what Jesus Christ had to say about it. We might begin by meditating on two images of heaven that Jesus proposed.

Heaven as a wedding feast. "Blessed are they who eat bread in the kingdom of God!" one of Jesus' hearers once cried out, and Jesus responded with the parable about the invited guests who take care of their own business rather than come to the wedding feast of the king's son. Their places are then taken by the poor, crippled, blind, lame, and by strangers on the highways and byways (Lk 14:15-24).

When the Lord described heaven as a wedding feast, he chose one of our most common experiences of delight. Middle Eastern weddings were a time of terrific food, including the delicacies of meat and sweets. The celebrations lasted for days as families were united in marriage and new relationships were established. Nor are such celebrations a thing of the past. I grew up attending Polish weddings that lasted two or three days, with great eating, dancing all night, and meeting relatives from my great-grandmother and great-great aunts, to newborn fourth cousins.

Christ invites us to imagine heaven as just such a festive and joyous event—a great celebration of a community, not individuals. Like the wedding that unites families, the heavenly wedding feast will unite all the families of the world into the one family of the adopted children of God.

Revelation 19:5-10 picks up the wedding feast imagery to describe the great victory celebration of goodness over evil. Babylon the evil prostitute will be destroyed, while the Church will be the holy Bride of Christ. Those who are good, whose righteous deeds adorn their souls like a wedding gown adorns a bride, will share in the feasting and rejoicing at Christ's great nuptial banquet. "Blessed are they who are invited to the wedding feast of the Lamb!" Blessed indeed!

Heaven, our true home. Jesus also spoke of heaven as the best of homes. At the Last Supper, he reassured his disciples that he would prepare a dwelling for each in his Father's house (Jn 14:1-3). Heaven is to be more of a home than any earthly home we have known!

In this new home the redeemed will be transformed and will share in the glorified life Christ has. No longer will they have bodies that cause pain and separation. In heaven, their souls will share in the most intense delight possible because they will see God, the most beautiful vision possible. Nor will this vision be something merely to observe. Each of the redeemed will experience absolute beauty gazing back at them with infinite love and total acceptance.

The life of heaven will not be the final story either, for Scripture announces the coming of yet another home, "a new heaven and a new earth" (Rv 21:1). Christian hope does not merely look forward to the life of the soul in a spiritual heaven. It also anticipates the life of the resurrected bodies of all the redeemed in the new heaven. The Lord Jesus Christ did not die just to redeem souls but whole human beings, body and soul. Resurrected followers of Christ will dwell in the exquisitely beautiful New Jerusalem, built of jewels and gold, a dwelling worthy of the glorified saints (see Rv 21:9-26).

CONSIDER THE SAINTS

One good way to enkindle our desire for heaven is to read and study the lives of those who have already reached this highest of goals. The saints' struggles, failures, and amazing accomplishments will inspire us to use our best for God.

The Bible is full of these heroes for God. The teaching on faith in the Letter to the Hebrews praises the great saints of the Old Testament who were examples of faith and hope in God's future reward. They form the great cloud of witnesses surrounding the Church today (Heb 11:1-40). The Bible also presents stirring examples of martyrs—St. Stephen, for example—who have been victorious over the devil.

Church history, too, offers an inspiring spectrum of sanctity. Perusing Butler's *Lives of the Saints* will demonstrate the incredible variety of the holy followers of Christ Jesus. In fact, there is a saint for everyone!

We Jesuits read about the saints of our Order throughout the world. Every Jesuit studies the life of St. Ignatius Loyola, and St. Francis Xavier, because they founded the order and passed on its spirituality. I especially like St. Andrew Bobola, not only because he was Polish but also because he was not easy to train in his early years. His stubbornness was transformed into perseverance through suffering: St. Andrew was tortured more than any other martyr in Catholic history. His story offers me hope that my Polish stubbornness, which aggravated my mother so often, might also be transformed into virtue!

Some saints were holy and pious from their earliest childhood, while others were great sinners who turned from debauchery and crime to sanctity and charity. St. John of God was an immoral soldier who converted at age forty. He tried some personally extravagant acts of penance but eventually found true holiness by serving the sick and founding hospitals for them. On the other hand, St. Catherine of Siena was pious from early childhood. God used her to reform the papacy.

Patron saints belong to all kinds of professions. St. Peter is the patron of fishermen and St. Paul the patron of tent-makers. Other jobs and professions have their heavenly heroes among their ranks, too. Anyone can ask their patron saint for prayers, as well as study their life to see how holiness is possible in their particular profession. The courage of martyrs like St. Perpetua and St. Felicity, young mothers executed for their faith in A.D. 203, can strengthen today's young mothers to survive the loving martyrdom of raising children. Many modern mothers can find consolation in the story of St. Monica, who prayed for the conversion of her wayward son, St. Augustine. He had joined a heretical cult, shacked up with a woman for fourteen years, and worried his mother to no end. But she followed him from Africa to northern Italy in hopes that he would become a

Christian. Once he accepted Christ into his life, she could die and commend herself to his prayers.

Many saints—like Teresa of Avila, John of the Cross, and Francis de Sales—wrote books that can teach us how to pray. Other saints—like Francis of Assisi, Dominic, and Charles Borromeo—can teach us how to be part of Church reform.

Anyone who wants to learn how to acquire a skill goes to an expert in the field. Don't watch a video of me playing golf; I do not know how to play. Watch Jack Nicklaus or some other great golfer, and you will be informed and inspired! Similarly, if you want inspiration and practical knowledge about how to pursue Christ's goals, examine the lives of the people who give an example of sanctity in this life and eternal joy in the next. They are the best role models for every Christian.

GET GOING!

Once we embrace Christ's goals for our spiritual growth and the salvation of the world, we are in a position to confront the particular situations we find frustrating. Here are some suggestions for taking action.

Offer yourself to God. Ask God to help you offer yourself completely for his service. This is the theme of St. Ignatius' "Prayer for Generosity," which asks for the grace of total commitment to God and his people simply for the love and joy of doing God's will.

Dearest Lord, teach me to be generous; teach me to serve you as you deserve. To give and not to count the cost, to fight and not to heed the wounds, to toil and not to seek for rest, to labor and not to ask for any reward except that of knowing that I am doing your will.

The prayer's spirit of generosity assumes a lively awareness of God's personal love and forgiveness of sin, a discovery that God's love is "better than life" (Ps 63:3).

For St. Ignatius, this realization welled up from the direction of the Holy Spirit in meditating on the gospel details of the life, suffering, death, and glorious resurrection of Jesus Christ, and from his deep love of God developed in intimate conversations with the Blessed Virgin Mary, Jesus, and the Father. For us, too, prayer and meditating on Scripture can make us more aware of God's love and more willing to serve him wholeheartedly.

Set specific goals. When we face frustrating situations in our parish, setting goals for change is critical. In so doing, we define our desires and give direction to our choices and actions. Goals provide motivation that can energize us to seek solutions.

Each frustrating situation must be brought before the Lord with much prayer and reflection as we discern, "What is God asking me to do here?" With our ultimate goal of doing God's will firmly in mind, we identify specific goals for each situation, and the specific plans for action and follow-up.

Clarifying our goals and making them explicit helps us to evaluate whether or not they are good and provides criteria for success or failure. It also reveals discrepancies between our goals and our actual behavior; sometimes we indulge in wishful thinking rather than setting real, operative goals. Only if we consciously identify specific goals can we adjust or correct them or, if necessary, repent of anything that may contradict Christ's goals for the situation. Lacking defined goals, we lack the criteria for self-examination.

State your goals to others. Making at least some goals public is a help because it can add to our reasons for carrying them out. Publicly committing ourselves to work for some change makes it less likely that we will leave the task unfinished. After all, who wants to look like a fool or a coward? Our Lord Jesus Christ speaks of this dynamic in his parable of the man who started to build a tower but lacked the resources to finish it, and his parable of the king about to march against an enemy who had a larger army (Lk 14:28-33). The right kind of social pressure can be a helpful stimulus!

Admittedly, giving one's word in public is not as respected today as it once was. Years ago, the sanctity of marriage vows held couples together through thick and thin. Today, one out of every two marriages ends in divorce, many within the first five years. Many priests and religious break their vows and leave their vocations. Cynics expect politicians to make promises they will not keep. Still, Catholics who are seriously working for change will benefit from frequent reminders about their stated goals. With God's grace, we can live out our commitments even in this climate of broken commitments.

Keep praying. None of us who seeks to change frustrating situations and contribute to renewing the Church can afford to neglect regular contact with God. It is essential to stay committed to growing in our relationship with God, in faith, prayer, and all the virtues.

WHY I BELIEVE IN GOOD GOALS

For many people all this talk about goals sounds too obvious. Why spend so much time on a practice found in every business and government office?

I used to ask this question too. Then I was appointed to a six-year term as the superior of a Jesuit community. I had certainly not expected to be asked to lead this fine group of priests and seminarians (Even Mom said, "I never thought they would make *you* a superior!"), so I came into the job with some observations about a few problems but without defined goals for the group.

Of course, this fuzzy sense of goals was a weakness that did not go unobserved. One day the priest who assisted me challenged my leadership style, saying, "Now that you have tackled some problems, what do you want to accomplish? If you focus on crisis management, you will create your own crises. What do you want to do?"I was dumbfounded by the question. "What do I want?" I began to ask myself. "How does change come about? What is my role in effecting changes?"

Two approaches were immensely helpful to me: studying

goal-setting from a secular business perspective, and taking my reflections on goals to daily prayer before the Blessed Sacrament. The study of goal-setting taught me about the importance of goals and gave me techniques for defining them and strengthening my commitment. Prayer taught me that the Lord is the one who sets the goals and strengthens me to pursue them. Discerning what Christ wanted for our Jesuit community was the first step; conforming myself to his will was the next. Not that I did all things well, but I learned as I went, developing some useful skills.

Were it not for this valuable experience, I might well be tempted to apply the same crisis management mentality to the situations in the Church that frustrate me. When I am faced with these problems, my first inclination is to sound a trumpet and attack with a Charge of the Conservative Catholic Light Brigade: "New Agers to the left of me, inauthentic visionaries to the right of me, but onward charged the faithful few hundred!"

Attacking one Church crisis after another might feel exciting and valiant, but what exactly would it accomplish? Would it be a quick fix to get rid of a problem or an effort to promote genuine renewal? Would it further Christ's goal of unity in the Church or would it widen divisions? Whose vision of the Church would set a direction for specific actions? Would there be any guiding vision at all?

Remembering my six-year stint as superior brings me back to my senses and reminds me of what I really want: to seek and further God's goals, not my own; to journey toward heaven in the company of the saints; to offer myself (and my frustrations) completely to God so that all my efforts for change may be directed by him.

Wouldn't every frustrated Catholic—and the Church itself—benefit from adopting these goals?

Remove the Log from Your Own Eye First

"I don't go to confession because I don't have any sins to confess, really. I'm a loving person, and I'm basically pretty good. What would I ever say in confession?"

How many times have I heard people proclaim their basic goodness as a reason for neglecting repentance and confession?

And yet everyone needs to repent and reform their lives on a constant basis, because everyone, no matter how sincere, opposes God's values and goals to some degree. Perhaps the great saints are an exception—though, interestingly, they themselves do not seem to have thought so. In fact, the great saints always saw themselves as the greatest sinners, even toward the end of their lives, long after other people considered them quite holy!

The call to repentance is especially important for frustrated Catholics who are working for some specific change in their experience of the Church. One reason is that we are

often tempted to express our anger over frustrating situations by blaming and judging the people we consider
responsible.

Those of us who are consciously working for renewal in
the Church are perhaps especially prone to pointing out the
sins of those we feel are blocking, slowing down, or oppos-
ing renewal. Father Benedict Groeschel's marvelous book,
The Reform of the Renewal,[13] develops this theme, explaining that true renewal in the Church requires each member
to be about the business of serious repentance of sins.
Blaming others is a great dodge which allows us to cultivate
a desirable self-image while ignoring the reality of how we
are behaving.

But Jesus Christ our Lord insists on dealing with real
people, not idealized fictions. He asks each of us to repent
of our own sin instead of confessing someone else's.
"Remove the beam from your own eye" before dealing
with the splinter in someone else's eye, he instructs the disciples (see Mt 7:3-5; Lk 6:41-42). He challenges everyone
with the parable about a self-righteous Pharisee who brags
to God about his good deeds and superiority over a sinful—but sincerely repentant—tax collector: the penitent tax
collector is the one who goes home justified (see Lk 18:9-
14).

When Christ met the Samaritan woman at the well, he
gently brought her to repentance (see Jn 1:1-42). He did
the same with St. Matthew the tax collector, St. Peter, and
others; in fact, the Lord Jesus Christ still continues to call
sinners to repent, revealing our sins so as to reconcile us to
God.

Sometimes he uses difficulties—tragedies, failures, feelings of spiritual desolation or a lack of purpose—to get our attention. Frequently repentance comes during a retreat or pilgrimage, when we are away from the normal setting in which patterns of sin have developed and are more open to the Holy Spirit sent by Christ to convict the soul of sin. In many varied ways Christ keeps inviting us to believe his teaching, see its beauty, and reject our sinful ways.

REPENTANCE: NOT JUST FOR BEGINNERS

Why is repentance so central to the Christian life? The answer appears in the ancient teaching of the Scriptures and the Church: because initial conversion and Baptism do not abolish human weakness or concupiscence, which is the inclination to sin that results from original sin.

"If we say we have no sin, we deceive ourselves, and the truth is not in us," writes St. John, addressing not pagans but fellow Christians. "If we say we have not sinned, we make him [Christ] a liar, and his word is not in us" (1 Jn 1:8, 10). Though an apostle trained by Jesus, St. John still includes himself among those who have sinned and who "confess sins... so that he [Christ] might forgive the sins and cleanse us from unrighteousness" (1 Jn 1:9).

The Council of Trent declared that "concupiscence or the tendency to sin remains in the baptized; but since it is left to provide a trial, it has no power to injure those who do not consent and who, by the grace of God, strongly resist."[14] This resistance consists in an ongoing repentance for personal sin—what the *Catechism of the Catholic Church* refers to as the "second conversion," which is an "uninterrupted task for the whole Church."[15] The *Catechism* recalls the teaching of Vatican II that the Church embraces sinners and is at the same time holy and always in need of purification, and so incessantly pursues penance and renewal.[16]

Asking forgiveness is therefore "the first movement of the prayer of petition," the *Catechism* explains, citing as an example the tax collector's prayer, "God, be merciful to me a sinner!" (Lk 18:13). This petition for forgiveness is the prerequisite for righteous and pure personal prayer and for participation in the Eucharist.[17]

Neither guilt-ridden self-hatred nor denial of sinfulness is a healthy course. Our goal must be the true repentance through which we come to be known by Christ Jesus. The Apostle John writes:

> If we walk in the light, as he is in the light, we have fellowship with one another, and the blood of his Son Jesus cleanses us from all sin. If we say, we are have no sin, we deceive ourselves, and the truth is not in us. But if we confess our sins, he is faithful and just, and will forgive our sins and cleanse us from all unrighteousness.
>
> 1 JOHN 1:7-9

Repentance brings a deep self-knowledge, since it entails a reflection on our life, actions, and unconscious motivations. Such reflection can lead to an interior conversion of the heart (the *Catechism* emphasizes its necessity[18]) and to a wise understanding of the deep-seated motives underlying our exterior sinful actions.

This is important because typically, people do not leave off their sinful behavior just because they have confessed it. Even if they do not want to commit the sin or experience the guilt again, they may do so because of the pleasure they derive from their acts of vengeance, lust, gluttony, and so on. Self-knowledge helps us to discern these sinful desires and motives. It leads us to seek the help of the Holy Spirit as we ask ourselves some hard questions: Why do I commit these sins? What do I enjoy about my sin? What is the problem with this enjoyment or with the sinful act?

The full process of repentance is many-sided. It includes recognition of guilt, which means taking responsibility for our decision and actions. An expression of sorrow for offending God derives from a personal insight into God's majesty, his unconditional love, and his justice. A firm decision to avoid the sin and its "near occasions"—the people, places, and things that lead us to commit it—requires a strongly felt horror of sin that motivates us to avoid it. Repentance also includes a type of reflection by which we realize how we got into the sinful situation and consider how to avoid it in the future.

HELP FROM THE PSALMS

One good way to stimulate the process of repentance is to reflect on the psalms, especially those which the Church has traditionally called the "penitential" psalms.

Psalm 6 is noteworthy because it overflows with a spirit of true contrition and offers marvelous insight into the process of repentance. It opens with a prayer for mercy.

> O Lord, rebuke me not in thy anger,
> Nor chasten me in thy wrath.   PSALMS 6:1

The psalmist is not denying that he deserves God's wrath, nor does he see God as many moderns do—as all-loving and accepting, ready to overlook even the most vicious unrepented sin. God our Lord does not have uncontrolled outbursts of rage, but the human emotion of anger evoked in this psalm is an apt image for his rejection of sinful behavior. The psalmist offers three reasons for God to grant him a respite.

> Be gracious to me, O Lord, for I am languishing.
> O Lord, heal me, for my bones are troubled.
> My soul is sorely troubled.
> But thou, O Lord—how long?   PSALMS 6:2-3

The first reason for mercy is that the psalmist has already experienced so much pain and suffering, down to his bones and his soul, to the very core of his personality.

Like fear, pain often motivates people to come to God and repent of sin. The last time I got drunk was in college, when I knelt down to make an offering into the porcelain altar in my bathroom, followed the next day by a miserable hangover. I have not gotten drunk since then, and I have neither intention nor desire to make myself that sick again. The memory of that pain still motivates me to stay sober.

"Save me for the sake of your covenant love," is the

psalmist's second reason for mercy (verse 5). *Hesed,* the Hebrew word used here, refers to the love that exists in the context of commitment, of a covenant relationship. God our Lord is committed to the people of the covenant—a commitment the psalmist is depending on.

The psalmist's third reason for mercy is that he loves God and wants to praise him. "For there is no remembering you in death," he tells God; "in *sheol* who will praise you?" (verse 6). Portrayed in the Old Testament as a dark, damp prison with gates like a lobster trap—you can get in but cannot get out—*sheol* was apparently not a place of praise!

> I am wearied with my moaning,
> every night I flood my bed with tears;
> I drench my couch with my weeping.
> My eye wastes away because of grief,
> it grows weak because of all my foes.   PSALMS 6:6-7

The psalmist depicts the drama of his repentance in emotional terms. Understanding how seriously one's sins offend against God's majesty and goodness often brings on tears of repentance.

Many of the great converts of the Bible and church history have wept copiously at their conversion. Jesus Christ gave high value to such tears (see the episode of the woman who loved away her sins by washing his feet with her tears: Lk 7:36-50). St. Ignatius of Loyola considered the gift of tears a sign of repentance. He himself would weep often, especially at the consecration of the Mass, and he saw this as a spiritual consolation. In fact, his eyes became so damaged by frequent tears that his doctor ordered him not to give in to the gift any more!

> Depart from me, all you workers of evil;
> for the Lord has heard the sound of my weeping.
> The Lord has heard my supplication;
> the Lord accepts my prayer.   PSALMS 6:8-9

Psalm 6 concludes with a prayer of confidence that the Lord will hear and accept this prayer of sorrow for sin. Likewise, each and every sinner who comes to Christ can be equally assured of receiving forgiveness. As St. Paul, himself a repentant sinner, wrote: "God shows his love for us in that while we were yet sinners Christ died for us" (Rom 5:8). All can come confidently to receive the great reconciliation that Christ has won for the world.

Psalm 51, another great penitential psalm, also begins with a prayer for mercy. "Thoroughly wash me of my iniquity," the psalmist asks God (verse 4), evoking the image of the fullers of his day, who treaded clothes in a shallow pool of water mixed with lye. The psalmist asks God to stomp his sin out thoroughly, no matter how painful this cleansing might be.

> For I know my transgressions,
> and my sin is ever before me.
> For I know my rebellions
> and my sin is before me always.
> Against you, you alone have I sinned

what is evil in your sight I have done,
that you may be righteous when you speak,
you might be pure when you judge.
Behold, in guilt was I conceived,
in sin was my mother in heat.   PSALMS 51:3-5

The psalmist recognizes that sin is primarily an offense against God, and that it is rooted in fallen human nature since it can be traced to conception. Verse 5 presents the only instance in the Bible where a human being is said to be "in heat," a term reserved for animals in other Bible passages. The psalmist hereby declares himself sinful all the way to his roots in conception. For that reason, he offers another prayer for a thorough cleansing from sin that penetrates to the most inward thoughts and replaces guilt with joy.

Behold, thou desirest truth in the inward being;
therefore teach me wisdom in my secret heart.
Purge me with hyssop, and I shall be clean;
wash me, and I shall be whiter than snow.
Fill me with joy and gladness;
let the bones which thou hast broken rejoice.
                                       PSALMS 51:6-8

At the Lord's command, sin is blotted out. His indwelling presence causes a sinner to know again the joy of his salvation and "a willing spirit"—an interior willingness to be good (verses 11-14). As a result, he will teach others to turn from their rebellious ways, and he will praise God for his forgiveness (verses 15-20). "Lord, open my lips and my mouth will proclaim your praise!" the psalmist asks, recognizing that the very ability to praise is God's gift (verse 17).

Prayed by sinners throughout the last three millennia, Psalm 51 is still an appropriate prayer for forgiveness and a good description of the process of conversion. The other penitential psalms—Psalms 32, 38, 102, 130 and 143—are also marvelous prayers to help advance the process of conversion and develop a spirituality of repentance and reform.

EXAMINE YOUR CONSCIENCE

As the penitential psalms demonstrate, repentance is not some vague feeling of grief for being a bad person. Rather, repentance is a keen awareness that we have chosen to offend God and neighbor, that the offense is sinful, and that we need God's mercy and forgiveness and the grace to change.

To repent we must know what offends God and neighbor. Since we live in a culture that is vague about sin, we can benefit from prayerfully considering books that offer examinations of conscience. Some possibilities: *Together in Peace*, by Father Joseph Champlin, and *Confession: A Little Book for the Reluctant*, by Monsignor Louis Gaston de Segur. The section on the Church's moral teaching in the *Catechism of the Catholic Church* is another excellent help for an examination of conscience.[19]

Guidelines from the Old Testament. Of course, sacred Scripture contains the basic material for an examination of conscience. And what better starting point than the Ten Commandments, God's hit parade of favorite laws. They appear in Exodus 20:1-17 and Deuteronomy 5:6-21:

I am the Lord your God who brought you out from the land of Egypt, a house of slaves.

1. You shall have no other gods before me. You will not make for yourself a graven image or any likeness which is in the heavens above or on the earth below or in the seas below the earth. You will not bow down to them and you will not serve them because I, the Lord your God, am a jealous God who visits the iniquity of fathers upon children to the third and fourth generation for those who hate me, but I show covenant love to the thousandth generation for those who love me.

2. You shall not bear the name of the Lord your God in vain, because the Lord will not hold innocent the one who bears his name in vain.

3. Remember the day of the Sabbath to keep it holy. Six days you shall work and do all your business, but the seventh day is a rest for the Lord your God. You will not do any business, neither you, your son, your daughter, your servant, your maid, your beast, nor your resident alien who is in your gates. For in six days the Lord made the heavens and the earth, the sea and all which is in them, and he rested on the seventh day. Therefore the Lord blessed the sabbath day and made it holy.

4. *Honor your father and your mother* so that your days may be long on the land which the Lord your God gave you.

5. *You shall not murder.*

6. *You shall not commit adultery.*

7. You shall not steal.

8. *You shall not bear false witness* against your neighbor.

9. *You shall not covet your neighbor's wife.*

10. *You shall not covet your neighbor's house.*

Notice that these laws take the form of unconditional statements, with no allowance for permission to abrogate them. God insists that humans not resist his Law, since his purpose is that all people be holy as he is holy (see Lv 19:2; 1 Pt 1:15-16). The Lord makes this point immediately before offering the Israelites the Ten Commandments: "If you really listen to my voice and keep my covenant, you will be for me a treasure among all peoples, for all the earth is mine. You will be for me a kingdom of priests and a holy nation" (Ex 19:5-6). We can become holy by following God's laws too, provided we have the humility to recognize that the norms for sin and virtue come from God, not ourselves.

As you consider the commandments, notice which ones make you most uncomfortable. Where does the conscience begin to squirm? These are usually excellent places to focus self-examination, because the discomfort may indicate an area of personal sin.

Guidelines from the Sermon on the Mount. Another great passage to read and pray over is the Sermon on the Mount (see Mt 5:21-48), where our Lord Jesus' moral teaching reinterprets and deepens some of the Old Testament commandments.

> You have heard that it was said to the men of old, "You shall not kill; and whoever kills shall be liable to judgment." But I say to you that every one who is angry with his brother shall be liable to judgment; whoever insults his brother shall be liable to the council, and whoever says, "You Fool!" shall be liable to the hell of fire.
>
> MATTHEW 5:21-22

Christ wants Christians to search their conscience and repent of any acts of violence, both physical and verbal.

Similarly, he requires not just chaste actions but chaste minds: "You have heard that it was said, 'You shall not commit adultery.' But I say to you that everyone who looks at a woman lustfully has already committed adultery with her in his heart" (Mt 5:27-28). In this age when everything from breakfast cereal to automobiles is sold with sex and where pornography is rampant, this area requires close examination.

Speech is another area that Christ addresses. "Again you have heard it was said to the men of old, 'You shall not swear falsely, but shall perform to the Lord what you have sworn.' But I say to you, do not swear at all.... Let what you say be simply 'Yes' or 'No'; anything more than this is from evil" (Mt 5:33, 37). Telling the truth is the absolute norm for all speech, precluding the need for foolish oaths, such as "I swear to God!"

Frustrated Catholics who are trying to correct some particular problem concerning their life in the Church must pay special attention to the area of speech. All change and reform must be based on the truth of the Gospel, of Church teaching and discipline, and the truth of the actual situation. We must resist the temptation to overstate the faults and misbehavior of those we see as opponents. Neither covering up facts nor exaggerating abuses in the Church serves Jesus Christ, who is truth.

Christ goes on to specify how his disciples must view their enemies. "You have heard it was said, 'Love your neighbor and hate your enemy.' But I say to you, love your enemies and pray for those who persecute you" (Mt 5:43-44).

At times, we may be tempted to hate, backbite, and gossip about those who we believe have caused the church problems, or those who oppose our efforts at change. It is tempting to become nasty and mean to a priest who has been insensitive to our needs or who purposely celebrates the liturgy improperly. But Christ calls each of us to repent when we give in to the natural desire to get even for past hurts. Love for our enemies must be the guiding norm behind Catholic renewal and reform.

Guidelines from St. Paul. The various moral reflections in St. Paul's epistles serve as excellent examinations of conscience. Prayerful consideration of Ephesians 4:17-6:20,

Romans 5:6-6:10 and Romans 12-15 will yield much fruit, as will the well-known call to love from 1 Corinthians 13.

> Love is patient and kind; love is not jealous or boastful; it is not arrogant or rude. Love does not insist on its own way, it is not irritable or resentful; it does not rejoice at wrong, but rejoices in the right. Love bears all things, believes all things, hopes all things, endures all things.
>
> 1 CORINTHIANS 13:4-7

Often chosen as the reading for weddings, this text can be paraphrased into an examination of conscience for every Christian simply by changing each statement into a question.

Am I patient? Am I kind? Do I avoid jealousy? Do I brag? Am I arrogant? Am I indecent? (This especially has sexual connotations of the dishonorable and shameful.) Do I seek my own way? Am I easily stirred to anger? Do I make an account of the evil other people do? Do I rejoice in the unrighteous acts of my opponents, or do I simply rejoice in the truth? Do I bear all things? (The Greek verb, *stego*, can mean to bear, endure, or stand, as well as to cover, pass over in silence, or keep confidential.) Do I believe all things, especially those taught by Christ Jesus and his Church? Do I hope for all things? Do I endure all things patiently?

Frequent review of these questions, accompanied by repentance when honesty requires us to answer them in the negative, will help us become better tools in the hands of Jesus Christ the Lord.

HELP FROM VATICAN II

The documents of Vatican II offer valuable help for an examination of conscience—especially in *Gaudium et Spes*, or "The Pastoral Constitution on the Church in the Modern World." Here, the Council acknowledges the rapid and profound changes within modern society, while showing how the gospel remains the norm by which the world is judged. It scrutinizes the "signs of the times" and interprets them in light of the gospel, always trying to use language that is intelligible today.[20]

With its application of the gospel to modern society and its consideration of social as well as individual failings, *Gaudium et Spes* raises many points to ponder as part of our examination of conscience. Here are just a few.

Contemporary society places a major premium on personal freedom; the Council reminds everyone that freedom is not a license to do whatever pleases one, even sin. Authentic freedom allows a person to seek God spontaneously and come freely to utter and blissful perfection through loyalty to God.[21] *How do I use my freedom? Do I use it to seek God or my own selfish concerns?*

The Council defines the common good as the sum of the conditions of social life which allows social groups and their members relatively thorough and ready access to their own fulfillment. *How do I and my community take account of the needs and legitimate aspirations of other groups and the whole of humanity?*

At the same time, the person stands above all things, with universal and inviolable rights to the necessities of life:

food, clothing, shelter; the right to choose a state of life freely and found a family; the right to act in accord with the upright norm of one's own conscience; the right to education, employment, good reputation, respect, appropriate information, protection of privacy, and rightful freedom in matters of religion. *How do I contribute to making the social order and development work for the benefit of the human person? How do I contribute to the social order's constant improvement, founded on truth, built on justice and animated by love?*[22] *Does Christian reverence for humanity lead me to consider every neighbor without exception as another self?*[23]

Love and action for our neighbor are essential, but they cannot render us indifferent to truth and goodness. *Does love impel me to speak the saving truth to all people? Do I distinguish between an error and the person in error? Do I judge the internal guilt of another? Do I forgive any injuries and love every enemy?*[24] *Do I recognize the basic equality of every individual and work for human dignity?*[25]

The Council stresses the nobility of marriage and the family, emphasizing that a healthy family life results in the well-being of the individual and of human and Christian society. It points out some of today's major challenges to marriage and the family: polygamy (in the modern West, this is sequential polygamy whereby divorce leads from one wife or husband to another); divorce which destabilizes the family; free love or sex between unmarried persons; excessive self-love and the worship of pleasure; illicit practices in human generation such as artificial birth control; disturbances from modern economic conditions, society's demands, and population growth.[26]

The tragedy of the disintegrating family can prompt us to examine our own conscience: *What am I doing to support family life in general? How am I contributing to the life of my own family?* Parents should pay special attention to their responsibility for setting an example of faith in the home and for taking charge of their children's religious education. *Am I trying to teach my children about the faith? Do my spouse and I pray together? Do we pray with our children?* Families where the parents pray with their children at church and at meals, for instance have a 50 percent better chance of survival; families where the husband and wife pray together have a 90 percent better chance of survival.

Christian spouses will find further material for an examination of conscience by considering their call to conjugal love and unity.[27] Children can reflect on their duty to respond to their parents' kindness with gratitude, love, and trust, and to stand by their parents in hardships and old age. Families should consider how to share their spiritual riches with other families.[28]

FORGIVENESS AND BEYOND

A searching examination of conscience and deeply felt sorrow for sin are not enough to reconcile us to God. Indeed, because sin is such a grievous offense against the infinite and eternal God—an "abomination," Scripture calls it (see Lv 18:22; 20:13; Dt 17:1; 18:12; 25:16)—there is no way for human beings to make amends.

The Good News is that God did what we could not do:

he came to earth to reconcile his sinful creatures to himself. The Father "delivered us from the authority of darkness and transferred us to the kingdom of the Son of his love, in whom we have redemption, the forgiveness of our sins" (Col 1:13-14). Jesus Christ, through and for whom all things are created (see Col 1:16) shed his blood to redeem sinners.

Because infinite and eternal God himself is redeeming us, there is no limit to the saving reach of his grace. No sin is more powerful than the saving death of Christ on the cross. The only thing that can block salvation is our human refusal to accept God's free offer of forgiveness and adoption as children of God. Thus at any and every point of life, we can respond to God's call to repent and be forgiven—especially through the sacraments of Baptism (for those who are unbaptized) and Reconciliation.

However, the joy of God's forgiveness is not the end point. Our Lord calls Christians to express their repentance through concrete actions, such as those the New Testament describes. These lie at the heart of the Christian life and make fruitful its work of renewal and reform.

First, reconciliation with God necessarily calls for reconciliation with fellow sinners. Jesus our Lord stressed this throughout his ministry, most especially when he taught us to pray, "Forgive us our trespasses as we forgive those who trespass against us" (Mt 6:12; Lk 11:4). When St. Peter asked if he should forgive people as many as seven times, Jesus responded with the parable of the unforgiving steward (see Mt 18:21-35): forgiving the relatively small offenses that others commit against us is absolutely necessary for receiving God's immeasurably merciful forgiveness.

A second act of repentance is working to bring a sinner back to God. We should do this for love of the brother or sister who wanders from the truth of the faith and, more importantly, for the love and glory of God who desires their salvation infinitely more than any human can. The inherent value of this good act is enhanced by God's promise that it will also cover our own sins: "My brethren, if any one among you wanders from the truth and some one brings him back, let him know that whoever brings back a sinner from the error of his way will save his soul from death and cover a multitude of sins" (Jas 5:19-20).

A third act of repentance is simply to love. Repeating a teaching from Proverbs, St. Peter writes, "Above all, hold unfailing your love for one another, since love covers a multitude of sins" (1 Pt 4:8; also Prv 10:12). Love transforms the sinner from a self-centered person into one who puts God and neighbor ahead of all selfish desires. God, who is love (see 1 Jn 4:8), is the source of all love—just as he is the source of conversion and forgiveness—and he provides the love by which we love.

As these scriptural promises reveal, God desires to use a variety of ways to forgive our sins. Whether through our repentance, forgiveness of others, work to convert others, or our love of others, God has graciously reconciled us to himself through his Son, Jesus Christ, in the power of the Holy Spirit. Let us not hesitate to avail ourselves of this forgiveness. And to the one triune God be all the glory!

FOUR

If Not Bad, Then Busy

A friend once shared a very wise saying on the importance of prayer: "Whoever the devil cannot make bad,
he makes busy." He makes them too busy to pray, to
reflect, to spend time with loved ones, or time with God
our Lord. People who might not fall for temptation to
steal, kill, or covet their neighbor's husband or wife, might
become so busy doing good things that no time remains
for the one thing that is necessary, according to Jesus Christ
our Lord. They are like Martha, too busy with many things
to sit listening to Jesus, as Martha's sister Mary did. And
yet, said Jesus, "Mary has chosen the better part" (see Lk
10:39-42).

No disciple of Jesus can afford to neglect "the one thing
necessary"—especially not those of us who are trying to
deal constructively with frustrating situations in our
Christian life. Prayer is a channel of grace through which
God can change the problems, and change us along with

them. Listening to Christ, we can know his goals for each situation and receive guidance to pursue them.

As the Gospels show us, Jesus himself never neglected prayer; he delighted in it throughout his earthly life. As a boy Jesus, the Son of God made flesh, learned how to pray from Joseph, Mary, and the rabbis, using the words and style of Jewish prayer. Yet Jesus took this prayer to a new depth by anchoring it in his relationship to his heavenly Father. This relationship of God the Son to the Father is the source not only of Christ's prayer but of all Christian prayer at all times.[29]

Each decisive moment of Jesus' ministry was marked by prayer. Jesus prayed before his Father gave testimony to him at his baptism and transfiguration, and in Gethsemane before his suffering and death (see Lk 22:39ff; 3:21; 9:28). Jesus prayed before selecting the twelve apostles, before Peter's confession of him as "the Christ of God," and at the Last Supper that Peter, the chief of the apostles, might not fall into temptation (see Lk 6:12; 9:18-20; 22:32). Frequently Jesus prayed in solitude—in the desert, on a mountain, and at night (see Mk 1:35; 6:46; Lk 5:16)—in order to enter into communion with his Father and to pray for his people.

Prayer gave Jesus a share in the experiences of "his brethren," giving him sympathy with their weaknesses so as to free them from those weaknesses (see Heb 2:12, 15; 4:15). His words and actions flow from his prayer in secret and lead his followers to a deeper prayer life.[30]

The Gospels record some of Jesus' prayers during his public ministry (for example, see Mt 11:25-27 and Jn

11:41-42). With their expressions of thanksgiving, petition, and confidence in the Father, they are models for all Christian prayer. This is especially true of the "Our Father," in which Jesus taught his disciples to address, praise, and petition the Father as he does (see Lk 11:2-4).

Finally, prayer was integral to Christ's experience of suffering and death, the central act of the world's salvation. At the end of his last Passover Seder, Jesus prayed a long personal prayer to the Father for the disciples' safety, unity, and holiness (see Jn 17). From the Upper Room Jesus led his disciples to Gethsemane where he prayed, "not my will, but yours be done" (Lk 22:42). His last words on the cross were prayers united to his redeeming self-sacrifice. For all their simplicity, these "seven last words"—two of them quoting from the Psalms—have evoked deep prayer and meditation from Christians throughout the centuries.[31]

Prayer constituted a major theme of Christ's life, from beginning to end. Similarly, our Lord desires prayer to characterize the lives of his disciples in every age and place. In order for this to happen, however, we must have some understanding of the goal and purpose of prayer.

FIVE FACETS OF PRAYER

What is prayer? Perhaps it is most fruitful to consider this question from various angles. First, prayer comes from *God's desire for relationship with us.* A relationship with God comes at his initiative and as his gift. As Jesus said to the Samaritan woman, "If you knew the gift of God, and who it is saying to you, 'Give me a drink,' you would ask him and he would give you living water!" (Jn 4:10). The *Catechism* connects this passage to God's love and consequent thirst for relationship by defining prayer as the encounter of God's thirst with ours. God longs for intimacy with us and approaches us so that we may thirst for him in a reciprocal relationship.[32]

Prayer is possible only because God the Father pours out God the Holy Spirit through Jesus Christ the Son of God, both before a person starts to have faith and, more fully, after one believes. The Holy Spirit makes prayer possible: "the Spirit helps us in our weaknesses, for we do not know what we are to ask for, but the Spirit intercedes for us with unutterable groanings" (Rom 8:26). We depend entirely on God in order to be able to pray to God; prayer is his gift and he is prayer's goal.

Second, prayer is *a turning of the heart to God*. St. Thérèse of Lisieux describes prayer as a "surge of the heart; it is a simple look turned toward heaven, it is a cry of recognition and of love, embracing both trial and joy."[33]

Though the whole person prays, Scripture speaks of prayer taking place in the soul, the spirit, and especially in the heart. Decisions made in the heart are deeper than the conscious thought because it is the place of truth, one's hidden center (see Ps 51:6), beyond the grasp of reason and of other people. Only the Spirit of God can fathom the human heart and know it fully, and the Holy Spirit desires to encounter every heart. The heart must be close and attentive to God, or the words of prayer are in vain.[34]

Third, prayer is *the ascent of the mind to God*, according

to St. John Damascene. The operation of the mind in prayer makes it desire and find its greatest satisfaction in the truth of the orthodox Christian faith. Though sincere, personalized expression in prayer is healthy, prayer needs to transcend personal feelings and ideas about God and share in the truth he reveals about himself.

Spontaneous prayer has its place, but it is not the only kind of prayer, nor is it always the best form. Anyone is capable of sincerely expressing trite, superficial prayers, or prayers that contradict Christ's teachings about God. For that reason, formal prayer, especially based on the Scriptures and the writings of the saints, is important for instructing the mind and raising it to God in truth.

Fourth, prayer is *an act of the will* by which one freely chooses to submit one's will to God's holy will in communion with God. St. Thomas Aquinas describes this aspect of prayer as an exchange of love that marks the starting point of mystical prayer. Such prayer is neither earned or deserved but is always a gift of the Holy Spirit whose grace works on the human will.

Fifth, prayer is *the living relationship of the children of God with their Father, with his Son Jesus, and with the Holy Spirit.*[35] Prayer is not some mind expansion or state of consciousness but an interpersonal relationship with the Triune God. Feelings of peace, joy, and even ecstasy may accompany prayer, but prayer may be dry too. What matters is knowing God and being known by him.

Further, an interpersonal relationship with God includes the body of Christ on earth, namely, the Church. Communion with God—Father, Son, and Holy Spirit—

will include communion with everyone united with Christ in baptism. Prayer is necessarily relational and social for Christians.

ASK! THANK! PRAISE!

Another way to understand prayer is to reflect on the particular purpose of the three types of prayer which are part of the Christian tradition. Each one is necessary, and each has its proper moment.

Prayers of petition. Unfortunately, some Christians treat God as a spiritual dispensary of goodies for those who know how to manipulate the correct formulas of prayer. For this reason, prayers of petition are sometimes disregarded or ridiculed. Nonetheless, abuses are no reason to neglect this very important type of prayer. After all, the Lord's Prayer is composed mostly of petitions, and Jesus often made petitions to his Father. The issue is learning how to enter into prayer of petition with a heart and mind centered on God.

The essential element of petition is dependence on God—a recognition that for all of our intelligence, strength, and ability, we remain creatures who depend completely on our Creator. In this spirit we turn to God as the loving Father who both provides our daily bread and runs the whole universe.

Prayers of petition also require persistence, as Christ teaches in two parables: the friend who induces his neighbor to give him bread in the middle of the night teaches us to "knock, and it will be opened to you." To those who pray so persistently, the heavenly Father will "give whatever he needs," especially the Holy Spirit who contains all gifts (see Lk 11:5-13). We also have the parable of the persistent widow which teaches us the value of unceasing prayer and the patience of faith (see Lk 18:1-8).

Why does God sometimes make us persist in petition for so long? If he knows he is going to grant our petition, why not sooner rather than later? While much of the answer lies in the mystery of God's providence, we can appreciate some of the important effects of persistence: growth in faith and confidence in God and a clearer, purified focus on our desires.

Of course, we must know how to ask and what to ask for. The New Testament teaches us to ask in Jesus' name, basing our confident hope of receiving an answer on Jesus. This is what Jesus revealed to the disciples at the Last Supper: "Whatever you ask in my name, this I will do so that the Father may be glorified in the Son; whatever you ask in my name, I will do" (Jn 14:13-14).

From the New Testament we also learn what to pray for. In the Our Father, Jesus teaches the disciples to make petitions which cause them to depend on God. The prayer for the coming of the kingdom establishes God's primary goal as the chief goal of our prayer. "Thy will be done" is a prayer to accept not our own will but God's in whatever petition we make. It means, for example, not complaining about the taste of the "daily bread" we have prayed for, but accepting all gifts as part of God's will. (I have often had to keep this in mind during my travels, when my petition for daily bread has been answered in the form of local delicacies like roasted guinea pigs, barbecued pig ears, and peanut and pig tail soup—with the curly pig tails swimming in the bowl!)

St. Paul's prayers also teach us how to offer petition, especially for other people. "The desire of my heart and my prayer to God for them is for salvation," he writes of his fellow Jews who have not come to Christ (see Rom 10:1). Whatever the local problem or frustrating situation, this is always St. Paul's main prayer and desire—that the troublemakers come to conversion and salvation, that the kingdom of God comes into their hearts and lives.

This should be our desire, too. We would therefore do well to meditate on all of St. Paul's petitions and make them our own in praying for the situations within the church that we find difficult. (A few suggestions: see Eph 1:16-23; Phil 1:9-11; Col 1:3-6).

The rosary is also a great way to offer petition. I have made it a habit to pray a decade of the rosary on the way to class, asking our Lady's intercession for my classes, for the students passed along the way (especially those who seem to be on drugs, hopeless, or aimless), and for myself. Repeating, "Pray for *us* sinners, now and at the hour of our death," helps remind me of my own sinfulness and need for prayer, as well as the needs of others.

Practically everywhere one sees the same problem. Committed, believing Catholics are not just frustrated but heartbroken over the loss of faith among members of their families. Parents are especially distressed at losing their children to cults, the occult, and hedonistic living. They are grieved because, typically, these young people never received adequate Catholic instruction and do not even know what they are leaving behind.

With the help of their pastor, some sixty members of a Chicago parish have found a way to respond to this problem: they pray. Taking their inspiration and their name from the mother of St. Augustine, who prayed for fourteen years for her son's conversion, they call themselves the St. Monica Sodality. Members meet monthly for a novena, Mass, and religious instruction and agree to pray throughout the month for one another's fallen-away relatives, whose names are placed in a special box, containing a relic of St. Monica.

These men and women have discovered great comfort and strength in interceding together. They have also discovered that God answers persistent prayer. One of their favorite success stories concerns an eighty-eight-year-old grandmother who was received back into the Church after an absence of more than fifty years away—and just before going into a coma during her last illness!

Prayers of thanksgiving. When God answers petitions, the most sensible prayer response is giving thanks! In fact, we are always surrounded by reasons to give thanks. The beauty of creation is everywhere, and we receive God's bounty in many ways. Having food, clothes, and shelter, receiving forgiveness in confession, receiving Jesus Christ in Holy Communion—these are just a few of the everyday reasons for thanking God.

Even when we are petitioning God about our problems,

we would do well to thank God for what he is about to do. This is what Jesus did before raising Lazarus (see Jn 11:41-42). St. Paul, too, often begins and concludes his letters with thanksgiving, even though he is frequently writing to correct problems in the churches. "Give thanks in all circumstances," he teaches. "Be steadfast in prayer, keeping watch in it with thanksgiving" (1 Thes 5:18; Col 4:2).

This attitude of thanksgiving in and for a problem situation does not mean accepting it as fine just the way it is. Rather, giving thanks to God is an act of faith that recognizes his sovereign ability to overcome the worst situations and bring good out of them. If God can bring the salvation of the world out of the death and suffering of his innocent Son, then he can surely bring good out of whatever frustrating situation we may be encountering in our parish.

Giving thanks in all circumstances is a good way to stop complaining about problems in the Church. It also keeps us grounded in the reality of God's love and power, which makes us more effective instruments for change and renewal.

Prayers of praise. Praise is the form of prayer which gives God glory not just for what he does but simply for his own sake, because he exists in all his infinite perfection. Praise recognizes and rejoices that the origin and goal of the human race and of each individual is in God. Praise is the main activity of the redeemed in heaven, and by the power of the Holy Spirit it provides a way for believers on earth to share in the heavenly joy.

When St. Paul calls Christians to "exhort one another in psalms and hymns and spiritual songs, singing with grace in your hearts to God" (Col 3:16; Eph 5:19), he is asking the community to express their praise together. This builds up the whole community of faith, while also bringing the deepest joy to individual Christians. Reciting or singing the psalms of praise should characterize the liturgy.

Meditating on these psalms and also on other hymns and canticles of praise in the Bible can lift up our hearts, especially when we feel overwhelmed and surrounded by problems.[36] Additional food for meditation are the Church's prayers of praise: the Gloria and Sanctus at Mass, the short doxology (Glory be to the Father, the Son, and the Holy Spirit), and the Te Deum in the Office of Readings.

WELLSPRINGS OF PRAYER

Any Catholic who wants a deeper life of prayer has only to tap into the richness of the sacred tradition transmitted within the believing and praying Church.[37] The best source of this Tradition, which is passed on in the history of salvation for Israel and the Church, is the Bible.

Praying with the Bible. Prayer should always accompany our reading of sacred Scripture, so that a dialogue takes place between God and ourselves. "We speak to him when we pray," says the *Catechism*; "we listen to him when we read the divine oracles."[38]

Sometimes this Bible-inspired prayer is vocal, using words either in our minds or mouths. The Our Father is a vocal prayer, as are Jesus' prayers of praise and petition recorded in the Gospels (see Mt 11:25-26; Mk 14:36). One simple but profound vocal prayer from Scripture—and one which the *Catechism* recommends—is the Jesus Prayer: "Lord Jesus Christ, Son of God, have mercy on us sinners." This combines the Christological hymn of Philippians 2:6-11 with the cry of the publican and the blind men begging for light (see Mk 10:46-52; Lk 18:13). If repeated many times a day with a humble, attentive heart, the Jesus Prayer will not only increase our awareness of our need but also open our hearts to the Savior's mercy.

Praying with the Bible also encourages meditation, a more reflective expression of prayer. This is "a prayerful quest engaging thought, imagination, emotion, and desire" in order to deepen our faith, prompt the conversion of our heart, and strengthen our will to follow Christ.[39]

Meditating on the great events of salvation will nourish our wonder and amazement at God's greatness and love. Allowing the Holy Spirit, who inspired the Bible, to stir heart, mind, and will anew unites us to God. As we pray over the Bible, the spiritual realities of God's saving deeds in history can become real in our own life.

Finally, meditating on Scripture can lead to the wordless, loving adoration of Jesus which is contemplative prayer. It is an attentiveness to the Word of God, a silent love which seeks Jesus, and in him, the Father. Contemplation on the mysteries of Christ's life teaches the "interior knowledge of our Lord," which leads us to love and follow him more closely.[40]

Praying with the liturgy. The Church's living tradition of prayer makes use of words, melodies, gestures, iconography, and art—all of which find their most important use in the liturgy. Participating actively in the Church's liturgical prayer will elevate our own spirituality and nourish our private prayer. Deep spiritual growth develops from meditating on the liturgical texts and Scripture readings before attending Mass or receiving the sacraments.

Our prayer life will also deepen as we use the official prayer book of the Church, the Liturgy of the Hours (also known as the Divine Office). Priests and deacons promise to recite this prayer on a daily basis; however, the Church recommends it to all Catholics. Composed of psalms, Gospel canticles, short readings from the Old and New Testaments, longer readings from Church documents or the writings of the saints, and other prayers, the Liturgy of the Hours contains much spiritual nourishment.[41]

THE BEST TEACHERS OF PRAYER

No Catholic who wants to grow in the life of prayer lacks good teachers—even if one of his or her particular frustrations is the lack of good confessors or spiritual directors in the area where they live! In the Holy Spirit, the Blessed Virgin Mary, and the saints, each of us has the best possible teachers of prayer.

The Holy Spirit is the great interior teacher of Christian prayer, drawing us by his grace and teaching us to pray by recalling Christ. Even the simplest devotion depends on him, for "no one can say 'Jesus is Lord' except by the Holy Spirit" (1 Cor 12:3).

For that reason the Church calls upon the Holy Spirit every day, and especially at the beginning and the end of every important action. The traditional form of petition to the Holy Spirit is to invoke the Father through Christ our Lord to give us the Consoler Spirit (see Lk 11:13; Jn 14:17; 15:26; 16:13).

The most simple prayer, "Come, Holy Spirit," appears in the hymns and antiphons of every liturgical tradition. "Come, Holy Spirit, fill the hearts of your faithful and enkindle in them the fire of your love," is a Pentecost prayer from the Roman Missal. Catholics of the Byzantine rite pray, "Heavenly King, Consoler Spirit, Spirit of Truth, present everywhere and filling all things, treasure of all good and source of all life, come dwell in us, cleanse and save us, you who are All Good."[42] Offering these prayers is a good way to invite the Holy Spirit into every part of our life.

The Blessed Virgin Mary, by her intercession and example, is a great aid to our prayer life—especially since Christ gave her to his beloved disciple (and thereby to us all) as he hung on the cross. The power of her intercession is shown at the wedding feast in Cana. The importance of meditation is exemplified by her own contemplation of the great mysteries revealed to her at Christ's birth, his presentation, and finding him in the temple (see Lk 2:19, 33, 51) and by her prayer with the disciples during the first novena awaiting the Pentecost gift of the Holy Spirit (see Acts 1:14).

The Church's prayer to the holy Mother of God centers

on the person of Christ manifested in the mysteries of salvation. Marian hymns and antiphons express two alternate
movements: first, they magnify the Lord for the "great
things" done for Mary, his lowly servant, and through her
for all human beings (see Lk 1:46-55); second, they entrust
the supplications and praises of God's children to the
Mother of Jesus because she knows the humanity which
God the Son took on in her.[43]

The saints are a cloud of witnesses who have preceded us
into heaven (see Heb 12:1) and who now contemplate
God, praise him, and act as patrons for Christians who are
still on earth. The saints, especially those who are officially
canonized, share in the living tradition of prayer by the
example of their lives, their writings, and their intercession
for us. When they entered into the joy of their Master, God
our Lord put them "in charge of many things" (Mt 25:21),
making their intercession part of God's plan and good for
the Church.[44]

Many saints received charisms, that is, gifts of the Holy
Spirit, to become God's instruments for developing varied
spiritualities throughout Church history. Just as, by God's
grace, Elijah could pass on his spirit to Elisha and John the
Baptist so as to start spiritual movements for their followers
(see 2 Kgs 2:9; Lk 1:1), so have many of the saints passed
on their spiritualities to us. Different styles of prayer and
meditation have been taught among the Benedictines,
Carmelites, Franciscans, Dominicans, Jesuits, and a host of
others.

The Church recognizes the distinct spirituality of each
school as an important contribution to the living tradition

of prayer and as a guide for the faithful. Their rich diversity originates with the Holy Spirit, like a single light refracting through a prism, illuminating each facet with a distinctly beautiful hue.[45]

All of us can tap into this treasure of the Catholic faith by reading the spiritual writings of these great teachers of prayer. A few classics are especially to be recommended: the *Confessions* of St. Augustine; the *Rule* of St. Benedict; St. Bernard of Clairvaux on *The Song of Songs*; *The Little Flowers* of St. Francis of Assisi; *The Imitation of Christ*, by Thomas à Kempis; St. Teresa of Avila's *Interior Castle, Autobiography*, and *Letters*; *The Spiritual Canticle, The Living Flame of Love*, and *The Ascent of Mount Carmel*, by St. John of the Cross; the *Spiritual Exercises, Letters*, and *Autobiography* of St. Ignatius of Loyola.[46]

MORE HELPS TO PRAYER

Fortunately, there are also flesh-and-blood teachers of prayer that we can learn from. Men and women who are living a consecrated religious life and who are sustained by their own prayer can teach the rest of us at their retreat houses, monasteries, convents, and other religious institutions. Prayerful bishops, priests, and deacons can instruct us through their words in the liturgy, homilies, and other teaching occasions.

The *Catechism* also recommends prayer groups as "schools of prayer" and as signs and driving forces for the renewal of prayer in the Church. Whether charismatic,

Marian, or one of many other types, such groups are aids to prayer if "they drink from authentic wellsprings of Christian prayer" and show concern for union with the Church.[47] Prayer groups should first become immersed with sacred Scripture and the classics of prayer and spirituality before experimenting with untested (or even rejected) spiritual writers, visionaries, and mystics.

Many Catholics have taken a positive step in their spiritual life and are dealing with their frustrations by starting or attending such prayer groups. A group of young adults at a parish situated in an affluent neighborhood of Chicago pray the rosary and some Scripture passages every Tuesday night. Many people in parishes across the country simply pray the rosary together at the end of Mass. Others pray the Liturgy of the Hours.

In some cases, prayer groups meet in homes—either by choice or because their pastor does not welcome their initiatives. Instead of complaining about the situation, they have learned to use it. A small group of women in the Archdiocese of Perth, Australia, has helped begin over three hundred Marian prayer groups. Some have a few dozen members while others comprise single families, but each is a source of strength and a stimulus to private prayer.

Of course, many pastors are only too happy to open the church doors to Catholics who want to pray. The church, after all, is the house of God and therefore the proper place for liturgical prayer. It is also "the privileged place for adoration of the real presence of Christ in the Blessed Sacrament" in personal prayer.[48] By God's grace, a movement to institute adoration of the Blessed Sacrament is gaining momentum. Fr. Martin Lucia has been preaching perpetual adoration in hundreds of parishes and has founded a small community called the Missionaries of the Blessed Sacrament to spread that ministry.[49] The effects of this prayer on parish life are fantastic: conversions, deeper prayer, and greater commitment to mission and service.

Archbishop Fulton Sheen had a marvelous insight that in Gethsemane, our Blessed Lord asked one thing of his newly ordained apostles—to spend an hour with him (see Mt 26:38, 40-41; Mk 14:34, 37-38). Spending an hour before Christ in the Blessed Sacrament transforms prayer and ministry, because the One who speaks through the prophets and who is speaking in the New Testament is the Word incarnate, body and soul, humanity and divinity, present in the most holy Sacrament of the altar.

Being before the Blessed Sacrament is very important in my own prayer. I love being in our Lord's presence. Praying before the Blessed Sacrament helps me grow in respect for the Sacrament and in a hunger for Jesus Christ. When I take the Scriptures before Christ, I read them more seriously because I know that the One in whose presence I am is the One who inspired the Scriptures and who is being written about in them.

Of course, the church is not the only place for prayer. The family—a "domestic church" by virtue of the sacramental nature of marriage[50]—should also be a place where prayer is not only encouraged but actively taught. To facilitate this, some people set up a "prayer corner" at home, with the sacred Scriptures and icons in prominent places, in order to pray in secret before our Father (see Mt 6:6). This kind of prayer room may foster private and common prayer in a family, just as a recreation room fosters fun. Families can gather there to pray the rosary or the Liturgy of the Hours, which divides the day into specific times of prayer, each with texts conveniently arranged for the day and season of the year. Fifteen minutes of Morning Prayer before leaving for work, fifteen minutes of Evening Prayer at the end of the work day, and five minutes of Night Prayer before bed will be more effective than hours on the couch watching foolish or mindless television programs.

Prayer may also be fostered by visiting Christian shrines. Pilgrimages remind us that life on earth is a journey toward heaven. By visiting the Holy Land, where the events of sacred Scripture happened, or other places made holy by various saints, apparitions, and other great signs, pilgrims find a renewal in prayer through contact with living the forms of Christian prayer "in Church."[51]

EFFECTS OF PRAYER

Over time, prayer matures and deepens. We speak less and listen more. Instead of telling God how to run the world and solve our problems, we ask him what he wants us to do. Instead of asking to receive things, we offer ourselves to his service. We are drawn closer to the Father, through the Son, by the power of the Holy Spirit. We grow in devotion to Jesus our Lord and are more strongly motivated to love him. As a result, we experience a greater sense of peace, integrity, and reflectiveness. We receive wisdom for dealing with situations that frustrate and grieve us.

The way we pray will change over time. Different circumstances call for different prayer methods. Sometimes we will be drawn to offer praise and thanksgiving, sometimes lamentation, and other times petition. But whatever the season, whatever the situation, we will experience the truth of St. John Damascene's assertion: "It is simply impossible to live the Christian life without prayer."

FIVE

Clever as Serpents, Gentle as Doves

Tony dropped out of the Catholic Church when he was seventeen. His parents had always practiced their faith with devotion, but their example alone wasn't enough for Tony. He needed answers not just about *what* Catholics believe and do but about *why* they believe and do them. His parents could not explain those reasons, and so, not finding the intellectual supports he needed, Tony drifted away. Finally, in his mid-twenties, Tony met a young Catholic who impressed him both by his insights into economics and his ability to explain the Catholic faith. At his new friend's suggestion, Tony read a book on Catholicism—and he has not stopped reading on the topic since.

Now an active member of the Church, Tony keeps working to develop his understanding of Catholicism, and to integrate it with his reflections on career goals, social problems, and other topics that face twentieth-century Christians. "I think that many other people reject the faith for the same reasons I did," Tony says today. "They don't understand what they're leaving, and there's no one to explain it to them."

IT PAYS TO GET INFORMED

Tony's story is a good example of why it is crucial for Catholics to have a good intellectual understanding of their faith. The most important reason is to develop as full a grasp as possible of the life that Christ Jesus offers us.

We all seek to discover life's meaning and make sense out of its problems and pains. The Church, so rich in experience about how to live well, offers a wealth of wisdom that can guide and help all kinds of people at all stages of life. The Catholic faith has been described as a river in which a flea can swim or an elephant can drown. The simplest child or mentally handicapped person can find peace of mind in the faith, while its majestic mysteries overwhelm geniuses like St. Thomas Aquinas and Blessed Edith Stein.

Another reason for every Catholic to be knowledgeable about the faith is to become equipped to witness and evangelize. Many Catholics know their religion the way I know French. I can read and understand texts, but I cannot converse: my knowledge of French is passive, not active. Similarly, Catholics who have a passive knowledge of their religion can recognize it but do not know how to explain their beliefs. Without this ability, how can they obey Christ's command to "proclaim the gospel to every creature" (Mk 16:15)? And how will Catholic parents and others who are called to hand on the faith fulfill their responsibilities?

A related reason for knowing the faith is to confront and correct errors. When the Jehovah's Witnesses on your doorstep quote Scripture to argue points contrary to the Christian faith, you must at least be aware that they are not citing the Bible you know but rather their own peculiar versions of it. When a friend informs you that the Blessed Virgin has designated an Australian visionary as pope, or worries because Padre Pio prophesied "three days of darkness" as a chastisement for the world, it is helpful to share the truth: that popes are elected by the College of Cardinals, that Padre Pio never made such a statement, and that Catholics are to focus on the great truths of the faith rather than on secrets disclosed in private revelation. When you attend a religious education class in which your pastor denies that the Assumption of the Blessed Virgin Mary is a doctrine of the Church, it would be good to be as well-informed as the Chicago woman to whom this happened: she was able to point out paragraphs 966 and 974 of the *Catechism*, which clearly teach this doctrine.

It takes some effort to develop our intellectual gifts by studying the faith. But the results are well worth it—for us and for the whole Church. Just ask Lenny Alt.

LENNY LEARNS HIS FAITH

Lenny is a postal worker in the Milwaukee, Wisconsin, area, and if ever there was a frustrated Catholic, he was it. It was his own ignorance of his faith that frustrated Lenny most. So often on the job his Catholicism had been challenged by coworkers—Seventh Day Adventists, Jehovah's Witnesses, Baptists, Pentecostals, and others, who all agreed that the Catholic Church was the "whore of Babylon." They worried that Lenny took part in a denomination headed by anti-Christ popes teaching damnable doctrines. Why did he pray to Mary and the saints? Confess his sins to a priest? Worship the Eucharist?

Lenny had no idea. He had never attended Catholic schools, and had just a dim recollection of the weekly catechism classes that had been his only education in the faith. Vaguely aware that these attacks were off base, Lenny felt at a disadvantage, unprepared and unable to respond. Finally, he decided to take action by getting the Catholic formation he had missed.

Lenny hunted through bookstores for new and used books to help him answer these questions and attacks. He read books on theology, apologetics, and Church history. He bought tapes by apologists like Dr. Scott Hahn to listen to while he was sorting mail.

The more Lenny learned, the more he realized that the answers provided by the Catholic faith were excellent and wise. He shared those answers with his friends at work by writing down his responses to specific attacks. By the end of his first year of study, Lenny had produced an eight-page newsletter answering objections to the Catholic faith. It was the first of many. Friends and opponents began asking for copies, and today Lenny's newsletters reach about five hundred people.[52]

Lenny's decision to get informed has not only met his own personal needs for understanding the Catholic faith: it has led others to appreciate it as well. One fallen-away Catholic who had joined first a Baptist and then a Pentecostal church debated Lenny repeatedly and angrily. Lenny stayed calm and answered the questions. Now his friend has returned to the Church. Another friend joined the Lutheran church because he could not accept Catholic devotion to the Blessed Virgin Mary. He was impressed when Lenny showed him the evidence for Luther's devotion to Mary—from Luther's own writings! In all these conversations, Lenny has learned to express his Catholic faith forthrightly but without rancor, filled with information as well as respect.

Lenny also teaches other Catholics what he has learned. In his parish catechism class he helps high school sophomores and juniors to understand and defend often-challenged doctrines like purgatory. The weekly Bible study he leads at a friend's home begins with prayer and then examines specific questions about Catholicism, along with the relevant Scripture texts.

Not every Catholic who sets out to get informed will develop the same sort of teaching ministry as Lenny. But with a better grounding in the faith, any frustrated Catholic can feel more equipped to take action and more hopeful that this action will be wise and beneficial to others.

A LIFETIME TRAINING PROGRAM
FOR CATHOLICS

How can an average Catholic get a good grounding in the faith? Anyone who is willing to read and study can tap into a wealth of resources that will serve as a lifetime continuing education program in Catholicism. Here is my suggested reading list for Catholic training to help us become "qualified, equipped for every good work" (2 Tm 3:17).

Study the Scriptures. Heading my list is the Bible, for "every Scripture is inspired by God and profitable for teaching, for refutation of error, for correcting faults, for training in righteousness" (2 Tm 3:16). Scripture trains our minds and guides our behavior. As nourishment for the mind, the Bible is the divinely revealed source of the teaching necessary for salvation, as well as the norm for refuting false doctrines. The word of God nourishes free will by pointing out both sinful behavior and holy righteousness. The inescapable conclusion: every Catholic needs to read and reread the sacred Scriptures again and again.

But the Bible is not always so easy to grasp. Remember the story of the Ethiopian eunuch who could not understand Isaiah 53 until St. Philip explained it to him (see Acts 8:26-40)? And the remark in the second letter of Peter that some things in St. Paul's letters are "hard to understand" (2 Pt 3:15-16)? Sometimes I feel that way too. My personal rule of thumb is to make note of difficult passages and pass on to the ones I understand more easily. Frequently, another text will explain the difficult ones. Often the difficulty is clarified by the writings of one of the popes, councils, Fathers of the Church or other saints, or biblical scholars.

A good Catholic study Bible or commentary may shed some light. If possible, consider learning one of the biblical languages—Hebrew, Aramaic, and Greek. Local colleges may offer such courses for beginners. For those who do not have that opportunity, some popular commentary series might be helpful, such as the Navarre Bible, William Barclay's New Testament commentaries, or the Michael Glazier commentary series. I never look to any one series to cover all of my questions, but a variety of books may help with their various perspectives on a text. Certain magazines are very helpful introductions to Bible study: *God's Word Today; The Bible Today; One Bread, One Body;* and, for archaeological information, *Biblical Archaeology Review*. Catholics who are especially serious about studying the Bible may want to look into some of the courses available at colleges, universities, and workshops around the country.[53]

Dig into doctrine. The Catholic faith holds together extremely well, and it is important to see how all its doctrines fit together into a whole way of living and believing. The most current and clear authoritative statement of Catholic teaching is the *Catechism of the Catholic Church*. Tones of faith, love, and hope ring through every page, and it is to be hoped that the *Catechism*—which has sold very well—will be read prayerfully and meditatively by everyone who has purchased it. This reading can be enriched by consulting *The Companion to the Catechism of the Catholic*

Church,[54] which presents the church documents and scriptural texts cited in the *Catechism* in a fuller context.

Some of the most important sources quoted in the *Catechism* are the Vatican II documents, which are essential reading for any Catholic because they set the tone for the Church in the modern world. Being familiar with these works also helps us to discern which teachings and practices are truly in "the spirit of Vatican II" and which are contrary to it.[55]

Two English translations are easily available in Catholic bookstores. *The Documents of Vatican II* appeared right after the Council and contains the documents, plus introductions by Catholics and responses by non-Catholics. *Vatican Council II: The Conciliar and Post Conciliar Documents* is a two-volume work which is especially useful because it includes many other documents that followed the Council.[56]

More help for understanding doctrine can be found in the adult catechisms written by John Hardon, S.J.[57] He explains Catholic faith and morals clearly and succinctly, without beating around the bush. Another Jesuit, Fr. Kenneth Baker, has written an excellent and most readable three-volume work, *The Fundamentals of Catholicism*.[58] Each chapter is short but pithy and easily readable, which makes the book a good tool for personal and group study.

Braver souls can go on to Ludwig Ott's *Fundamentals of Catholic Dogma*. This is a difficult but rewarding book whose outstanding feature is the wealth of sources cited in the text and footnotes. Ott gives the scriptural texts on which Catholic dogma is based and also cites the official declarations of Church dogma from the councils and popes.[59] Ludwig Ott's presentation of Catholic dogma is logical and thorough, making beautiful sense of the faith and morals. Even a partial reading is beneficial. The book is also an invaluable resource for further study on the topics listed in its index.

Know your church history. A good way to break into this vast subject is to read an overview of Christian history. Two of many good possibilities are Newman Eberhardt's *A Summary of Catholic History* and Warren H. Carroll's *The Building of Christendom*, which covers the history of the Church up to A.D. 1100.[60]

Works by Protestant authors can also be very helpful as follow-up reading to give a fuller picture of particular periods. Protestant histories of the Reformation—especially when they include texts by Luther, Calvin, Zwingli, and other reformers—can give Catholics deeper insight into the disunity in the Body of Christ. A Protestant view of various medieval horrors can enlighten us about why some Protestants react so strongly against the Catholic Church. Just be sure to choose a basically sound book such as *Here I Stand*, a biography of Martin Luther, and to use discernment as you read.[61]

Some readers find biographies a more enjoyable way to learn about church history and acquire a good historical perspective. Lives of individual popes or kings can give rich insight into their historical periods. Saints involved in the great issues of their day—like Bernard of Clairvaux, Catherine of Siena, and Dominic—are windows into various historical crises and doctrinal disputes. (An extra advantage comes from learning how the saints coped with crises and frustrations and grew in holiness at the same time.)

No study of church history is complete without some knowledge of the writings of key figures from the past, most notably the Fathers of the Church. William Jurgens' three-volume work, *The Faith of the Early Fathers* presents short introductions to the Church Fathers of the first seven centuries, followed by selections from their writings. His indices are fantastic aids for looking up topics covered by the patristic texts. Johannes Quastens' four-volume paperback, *Patrology* is a more in-depth treatment, with fewer original texts but a fuller explanation of each Father's theology and teaching.[62] After sampling the selections in these overviews, you may want to choose a particular Father and read more of his writings.

Learn the art of apologetics. Even in this ecumenical age, many tired old arguments against Christianity and Catholicism are resurfacing, and the classic answers are still relevant. The average Catholic can therefore learn much by reading and studying some of the great Christian apologists.

C.S. Lewis and G.K. Chesterton are two twentieth-century apologists who stand out for their beautiful use of the English language and their deeply Christian insights into modern problems. Lewis, an Anglican, and Chesterton, a Catholic, were both outside the Christian faith for a time, and so they know how to address the concerns and objections of atheists and agnostics.

Lewis' *Mere Christianity* is a good basic introduction to Christian apologetics. Particularly excellent are his sections on the role of the natural law, the saving work of Christ, and the significance of his divinity. *Miracles: A Preliminary Report* superbly presents the arguments of atheists, dualists, pantheists, and others—only to just as superbly demonstrate their inherent illogic. Lewis' arguments against atheism are the clearest I have seen and can address the lack of faith of most modern atheists. *The Problem of Pain* examines the arguments of those who lose faith in God because of suffering—always a timely topic. Lewis' other books explaining Christian truths—among them, *The Weight of Glory, God in the Dock,* and *The Abolition of Man*—also make for profitable reading.[63]

G.K. Chesterton, too, is an apologist with a tremendous love of the English language and a terrific imagination. He excels at using paradox to develop the reasons for belief in Christ and his Church. Chesterton's books—especially *The Everlasting Man, Orthodoxy, Heretics,* and his autobiographical *The Catholic Church and Conversion*—delight the imagination with good humor, as they teach the power of the paradoxical thinking that underlies not only Catholicism but all reality.[64]

Frank Sheed is another Catholic apologist who is well worth reading. He and his wife, Maisie Ward, spent many hours defending and explaining the faith (soap-box preaching was one of their specialties) and training other laypeople to do the same. The couple also began their own publishing house and wrote books on apologetics. Frank Sheed's *Theology for Beginners* and *Theology and Sanity* supply clear, cogent arguments for answering objections to the Catholic faith.[65]

More help for understanding and defending the faith is available through Catholic magazines and journals. Catholic Answers, an organization dedicated to Catholic apologetics, publishes a magazine called *This Rock*. Another magazine, *The Catholic Answer*, edited by Fr. Peter Stravinskas, provides information about doctrine, morals, and liturgical practices with an aim to helping Catholics present and defend their faith. *Hands On Apologetics* is a new magazine of practical apologetics from Thy Faith, Inc. of Farmington Hills, Michigan. Very useful, thoughtful articles can be found in Dr. Ralph McInerny's *Catholic Dossier* and *Crisis*, and in Fr. John Neuhaus' *First Things*. *New Covenant* magazine mostly addresses charismatic renewal issues. *Our Sunday Visitor*, *National Catholic Register*, and *Catholic World Report* present news and information.[66] Few of us can keep up with all of these magazines, but reading even one or two of them regularly is a good way to stimulate our thinking about our faith and to obtain information.

Finally, help is also available from various Catholic organizations which have arisen to respond to opposition from adversaries to the Catholic faith. Especially well-known is the Catholic League for Religious and Civil Rights, which Fr. Virgil Blum, S.J., helped to found in the 1970s as a religious advocacy group. The Catholic League centers its attention on issues where the Catholic faith is being ridiculed or attacked.[67]

FULL CIRCLE FOR SCOTT

Our study of Catholicism should not be done in a vacuum. That is, as we read and think about our faith, we should also be listening to the sorts of questions that people are asking. Atheists, agnostics, hedonists, and other nonbelievers raise certain types of questions; Christians who attack or disagree with Catholic doctrine raise others. Many of these questions are difficult to answer, which is why we need to study!

In many of my discussions over the years, I have had to admit not knowing the answers to various questions. When I am stumped, I admit my ignorance but I also accept the challenge of finding an answer that satisfies both my questioner and me. In Scott Butler's case, this took some doing!

Scott grew up in a normal Catholic family in California in the sixties, as many troubling changes were sweeping the American Church. Priests and nuns were leaving their orders and dioceses in droves. Odd liturgical experiments were taking place at parish Masses. Religion teachers said you did not have to come to church every Sunday if you were a loving person the rest of the week. They said you did not even have to be a Catholic—that Buddhism, Hinduism, and Native American spiritualities were beautiful and equally valid ways to get to heaven. Scott sloughed much of this off for a time.

But then he encountered the Jesus People movement, which challenged him with claims that Catholicism was a pagan aberration. He discovered a nondenominational church that preached an exciting Christianity with lively worship. By contrast, his parish seemed to offer only a dull "churchianity" feebly experimenting with guitar Masses. Scott's frustration with what he saw as a lifeless Christianity, along with ignorance of his faith, finally led him out of the Church.

With great enthusiasm, Scott helped to start a new non-denominational outpost. About ten thousand young people passed through it and were evangelized. He loved it! With a former priest, Scott worked to reach Catholics by distributing anti-Catholic pamphlets around local churches. In his twenties he became a minister.

Somehow Scott ended up attending a lecture series on the sacraments which I gave in the summer of 1982. What he heard whetted his interest but did not answer all of his questions about the truth of Catholicism, so he chased me down every day for the next month. He would come to the beach and drill me with questions when I returned from swimming. The Eucharist, purgatory, prayer to the saints and devotion to the Blessed Virgin Mary, the papacy, confession—we hashed out each of these issues until Scott was satisfied that he understood the Catholic position on each one. Finally, Scott returned to the Catholic faith.

Being educated in his faith brought a new excitement into Scott's experience of the Church, for he has become engaged in a dynamic apologetics ministry. The Lord has used him to help bring five hundred Protestant ministers and seminary professors to Catholic Church membership. These people, too, had real questions about Catholic doctrine, and they wanted scriptural, historical, and logical answers. Because Scott had struggled with the same questions, he usually knew what to say. When he was stumped, Scott researched the issues and then shared what he had learned. Especially well informed on the topic of papal infallibility, Scott has become adept at debating it with leaders of anti-Catholic organizations from coast to coast.[68]

LITURGY: A SPECIAL CALL
TO STUDY AND ACTION

Both Scott Butler and Lenny Alt are good examples of formerly frustrated Catholics who are using their hard-earned knowledge to explain Catholicism to those outside the faith. But the Church also needs well-informed members who can witness to the truth and accurately represent the faith to those *inside* it! Hardly anywhere is this need more critical than in the area of the liturgy.

It is not just that people's experience of the liturgy is the source of so many of their frustrations with the Church. It is, rather, that the very life of faith is at stake here. An ancient principle states, *lex orandi, lex credendi:* the law of praying is the law of believing. One aspect of this principle is that the phrases people use in their prayers express what they believe. Words are important. Change the formulas and phrases that people use when they pray, and you will also gradually change what they believe. Feminist forces in the Church have been quite conscious of this fact for some time, and their efforts are having an effect in liturgies across the country.

Rare is the Catholic who does not have personal

experience of these innovations. I experienced difficulties at Mundelein College when two Sisters from campus ministry asked me to celebrate a regular weekend Mass for the students but then objected because I called God "Father" when I read the Gospel from John 17. I insisted that I could not change the text; I had not written it and my role is to be faithful to it, not compose it anew. Furthermore, addressing God as Father is pretty much the point of that passage. The Sisters fired me. For the same reason, they also fired the next Jesuit priest to celebrate those Masses, though he died just before his final Mass with them. (Now their college has become absorbed into Loyola University.)

But many celebrants today cannot see the letters F-A-T-H-E-R without reading "Parent" or "Father-Mother." Other priests or lectors see the letters L-O-R-D and cannot help but say "God" instead, because "Lord" is a gender-specific term. Congregations are taught not to say "his" or "he" when referring to God in the Mass prayers; they clumsily substitute "God."

Certain Catholics push back patriarchal oppression by beginning their prayers, "In the Name of the Creator, the Redeemer, and the Sanctifier. Amen." Of course, this new formula lends itself to praying to the three functionaries in one God rather than three Persons. Furthermore, it does not accurately reflect the truth that all of God's functions outside the Blessed Trinity are properly actions of all three Persons. Neither does it recognize that all three functions depend on the existence of the creation: What was the first functionary before there was a creation? What was the second functionary before there were sinners to redeem? What was the third functionary before there were spiritual beings to sanctify? This is just one example of how a feminist politicization of one of the shortest prayers in Catholicism can have tremendous effects on theology.

In the Catholic Church the liturgy is the main arena in which one experiences the *lex orandi*. The liturgy is legislated by the church hierarchy so that it complies with the *lex credendi* and expresses the Catholic faith that comes from the apostles. Its roots are grounded in the ancient Church, and so it reflects the faith of the centuries.

The problem is that both small and flagrant abuses have become common in many parishes, retreat houses, and communities of religious. Sometimes these abuses come from innocent ignorance about the liturgy. Other times they are consciously designed to change the law of praying precisely to change the way people believe. Some liturgists admit that they are trying to "model the Church of the future."

A nun nicknamed "panty-hose Rose" because of her high hemline invited a group of seminarians to her apartment for Mass. Her home-baked loaf of bread was consecrated, broken, and eaten, with crumbs falling all over the floor. The seminarians were especially appalled when she pulled out her Hoover and swept up the crumbs! I cannot remember my mother (or any other hostess) vacuuming the rug while guests were still present. It is hard not to believe that her actions implied that the fallen crumbs were no longer the Body of Christ, a direct contradiction of Catholic doctrine.

Similar goals appear in retreats and meetings where a

priest and a woman stand in the center of a room or chapel to lead a community in the Mass. Small groups are seated around the chapel, with bread and wine. As the priest and woman say the words of the consecration together, a woman in each group holds the bread or cup in the air to let the priest's words of consecration hit them and change them into the Body and Blood of Christ.

TRUE GOALS FOR LITURGICAL RENEWAL

What does one do about liturgical innovations, abuses, or problems? Again, I suggest getting informed. Get copies of the liturgical books and norms and study them. The Church's documents on liturgy are public information available to anyone. You might consult *The Liturgy Documents,* Austin Flannery's collection of Vatican II documents (cited above in the reading list of works on doctrine), and *Inaestimabile Donum,* by Pope John Paul II.[69]

Since so many liturgical changes are claimed to be "in the spirit of Vatican II," give special attention to Vatican II's "Constitution on Sacred Liturgy" *(Sacrosanctum Concilium).* In its opening paragraph you will find a clear statement of the Council's four goals for liturgical renewal: to intensify the daily growth of Catholics in Christian living; to make church practices which are adaptable more responsive to the requirements of modern times; to nurture whatever can contribute to the unity of all who believe in Christ; and to strengthen those aspects of the Church which can help summon all humanity into her embrace.[70]

While all four of these goals should be considered prayerfully, the second one merits particular attention, since it is perhaps the one which is most often invoked to justify liturgical innovations. *To adapt the adaptable elements of the liturgy to the demands of the modern world*—this implies that the liturgy contains unchangeable elements instituted by God and changeable elements which have crept in over time. The former cannot be changed, the Council maintains. The latter should be changed if they are not sufficiently harmonious with the intimate nature of the liturgy or have grown less functional. The goal of making changes is to help Christian people understand the rites with ease and take part in them fully and actively, as befits a community.[71]

The Vatican II document spells out how these changes are to be made, insisting that the regulation of the sacred liturgy belongs to the proper Church authorities: in the first place, the Apostolic See, then, as laws may determine, the local bishop or competent bodies of bishops. "Therefore, absolutely no other person, not even a priest, may add, remove, or change anything in the liturgy on his own authority."[72] Innovations like having the people recite the prayer, "Through him, with him, and in him..." cannot be instituted by the local priest or congregation. Neither may they omit the Gloria or Creed, or substitute some other creed for the Nicene Creed or Apostles' Creed, both of which are approved for the Catholic liturgy.

Furthermore, innovations should not be introduced, even by the legitimate authorities, unless the good of the Church genuinely requires them. Also, any new forms should grow organically from existing forms rather than be created out of whole cloth.[73] The reason for this is that the liturgical services are not private functions. No Mass is the priest's Mass or the community's Mass. Each liturgy is a celebration of the whole Church, which affects and pertains to the whole mystical body of Christ.

Catholics who are frustrated by unsatisfying liturgies will be especially interested in what the Vatican Council presents as norms for the liturgy. The rites should have a noble simplicity, be short, clear, and unencumbered by useless repetitions. Each celebration should include more reading from Scripture, with more variety and suitability of the texts to the feasts. Preachers should treat the sermon as integral to the liturgy, preparing it by prayer and study so that the faith is proclaimed with exactitude and fidelity. Sermon themes and content should come mainly from Scripture and liturgical sources instead of the most recently popular movie. (One mother described an "E.T. Mass" based on the Spielberg film!) The sermon is meant to be a proclamation of God's wonderful works in history—especially the mystery of Christ— rather than jokes, movie reviews, or personal stories.

Something I never heard in the seminary is that Vatican II recommended the use of Latin in the liturgy! But it did, especially for Latin rite Catholics, while also recognizing the advantages of the vernacular languages and extending their use.[74] This means that Catholics who want to sing the responses and ordinary parts of Mass in Latin belong to the mainstream of Vatican II just as much as those who love the English liturgy.

The Council also made it clear that the Church does not seek to impose a rigid uniformity on the liturgy around the world. Thus, in Fiji, where it is considered impolite and arrogant to hold one's head higher than the head of a superior, Catholics sit during the Gospel with their heads bowed. However, the Council explicitly insisted that these rites may not be bound up with superstition or error; they should harmonize with the true and authentic spirit of the liturgy.[75] People who want to introduce ceremonies from Wiccan (witchcraft) covens into the liturgy—the "spiral dance," for instance, or the offering of incense to the spirits of the four directions—need to be reminded of this section of Vatican II.[76]

WISDOM IN ACTION

Once we have learned the Church's mind on the liturgy through study of its statements and documents, we are in a better position to work for change when we encounter the particular frustration of abuses and shortcomings in our local liturgies. These actions generally fall into one of two categories: correcting abuses and promoting positive changes.

Taking aim at abuses. A number of Catholics have taken action by forming organizations to combat liturgical abuses. One of these is CREDO, a society of priests dedicated to promoting "a faithful and reverent translation of the liturgy from the Latin."[77] Concerned that contemporary attempts to make the liturgical texts more "relevant" and "gender-inclusive" will compromise basic doctrine, CREDO works both to communicate its views to the appropriate authorities and to produce its own translations.

Adoremus is a primarily lay association with a somewhat broader goal: to "rediscover and restore the beauty, the holiness, the power of the Church's rich liturgical tradition while remaining faithful to an organic, living process of growth."[78] The association arose out of many Catholics' frustrating thirty years' experience of not seeing the liturgical reforms of the Second Vatican Council widely implemented. In too many parishes, beautiful music and art were replaced with poor music and banners; an emphasis on community and feeling replaced the sacred and sacrificial character of the Mass.

Adoremus is addressing the problem of uninspiring non-Vatican II liturgies in several ways. First, the association wants to provide sound liturgical materials to priests, seminarians, and the laity so as to promote beauty, holiness, and reverence in worship. It wants to assist bishops and the Holy See with scholarly analysis of the liturgical reform. When and where it is necessary, it will offer a critique of present and proposed liturgical practices. In addition, it publishes the "Adoremus Bulletin" to educate readers about Catholic liturgy and its history, about liturgical abuses, and to work on developing strategies to create a true renewal of the reform and deal with aberrations.[79]

Some Catholics have formed local watchdog organizations for noting (and even videotaping) specific liturgical abuses in their parishes and sending their information to the proper church authorities. Newsletters chronicling liturgical and other forms of abuse have sprung up around the country. They name the persons, places, dates, and events in a public forum that at times has a larger readership than the diocesan newspaper.

These watchdog organizations do have their positive effects. They help many average parishioners to become better informed about the Church's teaching on the liturgy. The publicity they stir up may encourage some church authorities to take quicker action than they otherwise would to correct liturgical abuses; it may also discourage some people from promoting such abuses. When a priest knows that he will be named, photographed, or videotaped while performing an odd liturgical dance, he just might choose to be a wallflower.

On the negative side, however, the human tendency to report only the sensational and look for as much dirt as possible sometimes results in inaccuracies, overstatements, and rash judgments. Not uncommonly, the authors of muckraking articles do not speak to the persons involved directly, and they may misunderstand the situation or attribute to them wrong motives. Sometimes writers do not report events accurately. The problem is that such mistakes may ruin someone's reputation in the community.

While some occasional public whistle-blowing may be necessary, perhaps a better approach in general is to deal with offenders more directly. I admire those Catholic women who attend feminist conferences or small groups and contest the heretical statements frankly and plainly. Calling St. Monica a b____ or celebrating a feminist liturgy gets challenged on the spot, despite the outburst this action may provoke. In general, documenting an abuse and then speaking directly to the offender, or the immediate superiors if necessary, is better than informing the public.

Promoting positive change. Catholics whose study of the liturgy has brought them to a deeper love and understanding of it can have a ripple effect on those around them. If they communicate to their fellow parishioners—even informally—something of their findings and their enthusiasm, they will be helping to create a broader base of support for liturgical renewal.

One obvious way to take positive steps for the liturgy is to get involved in the parish liturgy committee. Training and education in the liturgical documents, sacred music, and the history of the liturgy are tremendous preparations for this type of work. When fellow committee members learn that you are serious, well-informed, and creative, they will probably pay attention to your suggestions. When your own devotion is deep and your prayer profound, you will bring a silent but real quality that can infect the rest of the committee with a desire to worship God, teach the Catholic faith, and evangelize non-believers.

Another positive step is to encourage and participate in whatever local activities promote true liturgical awareness and renewal. One such activity is a parish Bible service. Especially fitting in Advent and Lent and on Sundays and feast days, these services are helpful supplements to the evangelical proclamation of the liturgy.[80] Supporting them (or suggesting them, if you are on the parish liturgy committee) is a good way to further positive change.

A greater appreciation for the liturgy can also be fostered by participating in a prayer group, whether Marian, charismatic, or of another type. Through such movements, thousands of people have turned from lives of sin or neglect of the faith to a lively commitment to Christ and the Church. Commitment to a prayer group usually deepens personal conversion, devotion, and hunger for prayer. It encourages both private prayer and sacramental life. Prayer group attendees become more sincere Mass attendees. This type of prayerful conversion may be the most important action any Catholic can take to promote liturgical growth.

Here, too, a good intellectual grounding in the faith will be protection against some common problems. Like many other Catholics, some prayer group members do not know their faith well enough to discern theological errors (a weakness which can be traced to the decline of catechetical instruction over the last thirty years). They rightly react when homilists try to explain away all miracles—for example, by saying that Jesus did not really multiply the loaves and fishes but performed a "greater miracle" of getting everyone to share the bread and fish they had hidden under their cloaks. But because they are looking for evidence of God acting today, they may fall into the opposite error of seeing "miracles" where there are none.

Some Catholics who experience conversion through a prayer group are so surprised and even overwhelmed by the accompanying emotion that they reject the need for an intellectual component of faith. As a result, some charismatics end up seeking warm fellowship and biblical teaching in non-denominational groups.

Some Catholics in Marian movements are liable to follow any one of thousands of visionaries around the world because they see the sun spinning or rosaries turning to gold. Unfortunately, they do not always critically examine the truth of what certain visionaries say—for example, the claim of one visionary that a picture of Jesus is as much the Real Presence as the Blessed Sacrament. (A sacrament is an outward sign communicating grace and instituted by Christ, not by Eastman Kodak.)

Enthusiasm can overwhelm one's thinking faculties, good sense, and willingness to make a sound judgment of faith. But when Catholics in renewal movements are well formed in Scripture, theology, and history, their enthusiasm will be well directed and contribute to the reform of liturgy and many other areas of Catholic life.

God wants us to use our minds—to develop our ability to think, know, and understand the world and the truths he has revealed through Jesus Christ. As we do, we will grow in our faith and reach out to others more effectively. We will be better equipped to face our frustrations, deal with difficult situations, and contribute to reform and renewal.

SIX

Walk Through Open Doors

For better or for worse, every response to frustration affects the body of Christ.

Ignore your frustration and it will fester, impairing both your relationship with God and your ability to serve his people. Withdraw without making the effort to confront errors or fill voids, and the needs that you have seen may never be addressed. Pray and educate yourself on some aspect of church life or teaching that troubles you, and the wisdom and knowledge you acquire will also overflow to others. Face and resolve your differences with another parishioner, and you will build up the unity of the Church instead of tearing it down.

Sometimes our frustrations concern private matters, and how we deal with them has a hidden effect on our fellow members in the body of Christ. Other types of situations are more in the public eye. Responding to these in a healthy way can be of great direct benefit to many people—

sometimes to far more people than we might imagine.

How many frustrated Catholics have tackled some troubling situation, only to find that by doing so they have walked through a God-given door of opportunity and stepped into a ministry they had not sought or anticipated! Of course, the impact of our actions is not ours to determine. Our task is simply to live righteously, look for open doors, and leave the rest to God.

Even St. Paul, who was quite clear that his mission was the conversion of the whole Roman Empire, depended on God to lead him step by step by opening doors to ministry. "A great door was opened to me for work," is the marvelous image he uses to describe his start in the early fifties A.D., when he postponed his plans to visit the Corinthians and remained in Ephesus until Pentecost (see 1 Cor 16:9). A few years later St. Paul asked the Colossians to "pray for us also, that God may open to us a door for the word, to declare the mystery of Christ, on account of which I am imprisoned, and that I may make it clear, as I ought to speak" (Col 4:3-4). St. Paul's image of the Lord opening a door of opportunity for ministry recognizes the Christian's dependence on Christ's action as well as the need to discern God's will.

The image is developed in the book of Revelation when the Lord tells John, "And to the angel of the church in Philadelphia write: 'The words of the holy one, the true one, who has the key of David, who opens and no one shuts, who shuts and no one opens'" (Rv 3:7). St. John's vision shows the power of Jesus Christ to open and close the doors of opportunity.

Christians do not need battering rams to shatter all opposition to the gospel truth. Rather, we need hearts that discern which doors Christ has opened and which he has shut. When the Lord opens a door, the believer needs courage to accept the present opportunity. When the Lord shuts a door, the person of faith walks away peacefully, seeking the other openings which God will unlock.

A GREAT DOOR WAS OPENED TO *ME!*

I did not know it at the time, but one Saturday morning I walked through a door of opportunity and stepped into a career in the media. It all began while I was a Vanderbilt grad student.

A convert buddy and I were driving in Nashville, Tennessee. I had just bought a cowboy hat (my first since I was six years old), but my delight over this purchase was dimmed by hearing an anti-Catholic diatribe on the local Christian radio station. Frustrated, I decided to call the station manager and request that such offensive programs not be broadcast.

The station manager, who happened to be the wife of a fellow Vanderbilt grad student, said she was powerless to edit these programs, even when her own Pentecostal church was attacked. Since the preachers had paid for air time, they could say whatever they wanted. But she did invite me to be a guest on a radio call-in talk show where I could answer questions about the Catholic Church.

The host of the show, Ruth Ann Leach, was a wonderful

interviewer. She asked pointed questions in a gentle, open manner and her sense of humor defused potentially tense moments. We hit it off well and had a great interview. I only wished that my parents could have heard the show, since I thought it would be the sole broadcast of my career.

It was not. Ruth Ann invited me back a few more times, which inspired some local Catholics to collect money to finance my own radio program called *A Catholic View of Scripture*. We broadcast on the same Evangelical station, using both pre-recorded and call-in shows. The series was short-lived because the backers ran out of money due to a recession. The radio stint had been fun and served a purpose, I thought, but it was over. Besides, I needed time to write my dissertation.

A month later a Pentecostal television show invited me to be a guest on their first broadcast. I was thrilled and took the opportunity. Another Catholic guest on that show was William Steltemeier, the president of the then fledgling Eternal Word Television Network (EWTN) started by Mother M. Angelica. Bill liked the way I handled myself on the air, so he extended a verbal invitation to appear on EWTN. Nothing happened for ten months, when I was invited to be Mother Angelica's Sadie Hawkins Day guest on her live show, February 29, 1984. I drove down I-65 to Birmingham in my beloved but beat-up $200 1968 Pontiac LeMans, bought from my convert friend in Nashville. Wearing flack jacket, jeans, workboots, and cowboy hat, I drove into the EWTN parking lot. Mother Angelica and Sr. Raphael walked up to me and asked, "Can we help you, sir?" Enthusiastically, I answered, "Hi,

Mother, I'm Mitch Pacwa, the guest on your show tonight!" She rolled her eyes and hit her forehead, wearing a polite, weak smile. I gussied up in the guest house, let them put on make-up, and went to the control room for prayers. Mother was obviously relieved to see me in clerical shirt and black coat.

The show went so well that Mother Angelica not only extended it for an extra hour but also invited me to have my own TV series. I could not believe it! I readily agreed, and we made plans the next day for my return in May to do a thirteen-episode series on the Book of Psalms. A number of other series on the Old Testament, justification, and the New Age movement have followed. I have developed into such a ham that on the tenth anniversary show I asked Mother Angelica whether it was kosher for me to speak about the Old Testament. She hit me—on the air!

In the summer of 1986, I was asked to participate in a series of televised debates on the differences between Catholicism and Evangelical Protestantism. I had never participated in a formal debate before, but I was eager to explain the Catholic faith to as many Protestants as possible. Despite some problems in format, I consider this series a great success because it influenced a number of Protestants and ex-Catholics to come into or return to the Catholic Church.[81]

The television broadcasts opened more doors. Servant Publications invited me to write *Catholics and the New Age*, as well as this book. Magazine and journal editors ask me to write articles for them. Conferences and parishes host me as a speaker. Newspapers around the world have interviewed me. And all because I complained about an anti-Catholic radio broadcast.

My experience is far from unique. In fact, the rest of this chapter will introduce you to other Catholics who unsuspectingly walked through open doors and ended up doing media work or founding organizations that have touched the lives of many people. These are Catholics who saw a need and used their talents to respond creatively, as God led the way.

The point is not to try and duplicate their actions but to use the talents God has given us in our own way. Whether or not our responses to open doors have similar far-reaching effects, the stories of these Catholics should inspire us to persevere in the tremendous adventure of responding to God.

CATHOLIC ANSWERS FOR DEFENDING THE FAITH

In 1980 an attorney named Karl Keating found some anti-Catholic literature in his parish church in San Diego. Instead of merely clucking his tongue and throwing the tract away, he took it home and composed a one-page response. He ran off a few hundred copies and brought them to the church whose address was on the anti-Catholic tract. His response included a post box number and the name of a non-existent organization, Catholic Answers.

Karl forgot about the incident until a few weeks later, when he discovered to his surprise that the post box contained a couple dozen letters from around the country requesting more of his tracts. Not having any, he started to write them. Over time Karl realized that these tracts could form the core of a book. The result was his marvelously successful *Catholicism and Fundamentalism*.[82]

In 1982 Karl transformed the fictional Catholic Answers into reality by officially incorporating. In the spring of 1987 two other men joined him: Patrick Madrid, a salesman who was working on his own apologetics project, became an associate in apologetics, and Charlie Harvey began helping with clerical work. They moved their workplace out of Karl's kitchen into a small office and decided to defend and spread the Catholic faith by offering seminars, selling Catholic books, and holding debates.

Karl and other Catholic Answers staffers have participated in many debates since then, learning more about the faith and apologetics with each one. They have taken on former Catholics who are now Mormons, as well as leaders of anti-Catholic organizations such as Mission to Catholics (run by an ex-priest), Christians Evangelizing Catholics, and Iglesia ni Cristo, a Filipino group which denies Christ's divinity.

Catholic Answers debaters make it a point to be polite, not contentious; they focus on the topic rather than attack the person they are debating. Furthermore, each debate is a learning experience (every teacher knows that the best learning occurs when one teaches) and is prepared for by studying Catholic theology. To train other Catholics in defending the faith, Catholic Answers makes the tapes of each debate available to anyone interested.

A dozen people form the Catholic Answers staff today. They handle questions from callers, take orders for Catholic literature, and write articles. They also publish *This Rock*, a magazine that grew out of an apologetics newsletter started in 1986. Working for Catholic Answers provides an informed, solid Catholic foundation for its staff members, some of whom have moved on to exercise influence in other Catholic ministries.

Thousands of people both inside and outside the Church have benefited from Catholic Answers' ministry over the years. And all because Karl Keating took that first small step through an open door.[83]

BELEAGUERED CATHOLICS FIND RELIEF

A similar desire to combat error launched Charles Wilson into an unsought-for ministry that addresses abuses within the Church.

Reading the local newspaper on September 16, 1981, Charles learned that the Archdiocese of San Antonio was sponsoring an international Marian symposium in honor of the apparitions of Mary at Guadalupe in 1581. His initial enthusiasm waned when he discovered that the conference speakers included several prominent speakers and writers about whose liberal viewpoints Charles had significant questions.

"Someone ought to do something about this this!" Charles exclaimed, throwing down the paper.

"Why don't you do something about it yourself?" his

wife responded. Charles didn't relish the thought of extra work, but he knew she was right.

With the help of the *Wanderer,* a national conservative Catholic newspaper, Charles formed a group of local concerned Catholics to serve as an ad hoc committee to try to derail the symposium or mitigate its effects. When the symposium was canceled for reasons unrelated to these efforts, the committee decided to organize its own mini-conference on December 12, the feast of Our Lady of Guadalupe, Patroness of the Americas. About seventy-five people attended, enjoying not only the spaghetti dinner and lecture but also the chance to meet other area Catholics with the same concerns.

Inspired by this interest, Charles and a few friends formed the Fidelity Forum of Texas and went on to plan a larger scale international Marian symposium. Held in May 1982, this event was attended by four hundred people. As a result, Charles was asked to help establish similar groups and conferences throughout the country. This work opened his eyes to the great needs of Catholics who were pleading for help to combat problems such as liturgical abuses and inappropriate sex education programs. But the only thing Charles knew how to do was to set up one-day events without follow-up.

The promulgation of the new Code of Canon Law in 1983 became another open door for Charles. It inspired him by its insistence that Catholics have "rights" to true teaching and legitimate liturgy, rights which they can vindicate and defend "before a competent ecclesiastical court in accord with the norm of law" (Canon 221, section 2). But,

Charles wondered, how many ordinary Catholics would be able to defend their rights within the Church's legal structure without some professional and practical assistance?

It was to meet this need that Charles established the St. Joseph Foundation in 1984, with the help of Charles Rice, from Notre Dame University. The Foundation's goal is to direct the "beleaguered" faithful through the proper channels as they address grievances and seek their rights to the truth, liturgical norms, and authentic catechesis.

Charles realized that to be effective he needed more training, especially since he was a convert and did not have the advantage of years of developed Catholic education. To remedy the situation, he earned a Masters degree in theology at a local seminary (not without encountering opposition from some liberal professors whose opinions he challenged). He took every course offered in canon law and made that his specialty. Armed with his degree, Charles now uses the St. Joseph Foundation to offer hands-on legal assistance to any Catholic who seeks help for correcting problems within the Church. His staff now numbers two full-time and two part-time workers, including a priest canon lawyer; other priests and laity consult on a casework basis.

The Foundation's approach is practical, using techniques similar to those of secular law firms. All complainants must go through a screening process by fulfilling two requirements. First, they must pray and reflect so as to distinguish whether their particular complaint is a real abuse, requiring action, or a difference of taste and preference, requiring charity and forbearance. Second, all complainants are asked to weigh the rightness of their position against the good of the Church. In some situations it may be better to bear abuses, in others to vigorously pursue justice.

For situations demanding action, the Foundation helps to define the problem and collect documentation to substantiate the abuse. Then remedies are explored and a step-by-step resolution is undertaken, starting with a simple solution like an arbitration process. Usually a succinct letter to a pastor or an informal procedure resolves the situation. But sometimes the cases go as far as the Apostolic Asignatura, a Church court in Rome.

Charles Wilson would like nothing better than to go out of business due to a lack of abuses in the Church. Until the Lord opens that door of opportunity, he and the St. Joseph Foundation will continue their vital service to the Church.[84]

SEMINARIANS, UNITE!

It is not always frustration with abuses or errors that motivates Catholics to walk through open doors and into ministry. Some Catholics have simply noticed a need and set out to meet it creatively in a way that helps others. Here, too, it is God who opens the way and gives the growth.

Seminarian Jerry Usher and some seminarian friends have met many other young men who are trying to discern God's vocation and are seriously considering the priesthood. Very little in our materialistic and sexually gluttonous society encourages a lifestyle of chastity, poverty and simplicity, and obedience.

To offer this support and cultivate priestly vocations, Jerry and some friends felt moved to start a newsletter called *In Persona Christi* ("In the Person of Christ"). This is a traditional term by which the Church has understood the office of the priest as one in which he acts in the person of Christ while celebrating the sacraments.[85]

The newsletter has a clear mission statement:

In Persona Christi is published by seminarians, for seminarians, and for all men who are considering a vocation to the Roman Catholic priesthood. It is the will of Christ that his Church, in every age, have a sufficient number of priests to shepherd his people to salvation. In our day it is clear that the Holy Spirit is prompting men of all ages and from all walks of life to respond to this important call. With fidelity to the Church's magisterium, devotion to our Holy Father, bishops and superiors, and with a keen awareness that the hopes of the Church and the salvation of souls are being committed to us, *In Persona Christi* desires to contribute to the formation of men into holy priests who will bring forth abundant and lasting fruit.

To carry out its mission, the newsletter offers a variety of material. It presents explanations of the scriptural foundations for Catholic beliefs, discussions of moral and pastoral situations, the teachings of Church Fathers, and features on saints. Interviews with seminarians, priests, and bishops recount their vocation stories. The newsletter includes news of events at various seminaries and even a comic strip about the lighter side of seminary life.

Now reaching seminarians and potential seminarians around the country, *In Persona Christi* is strengthening them in their common goal of service to Christ and his Church as priests, with a clear commitment to the official teachings of the Church. For some readers, this vehicle of shared love for Christ and his Church is a major support for choosing and pursuing the path to ordination.[86]

A FUTURE FULL OF HOPE

Fr. Peter Stravinskas saw another need, which he expressed to two editor friends at the 1985 Catholic Press Association convention. "What do you see for the future?" one of them had asked him. "We are on the brink of a Catholic restoration," Fr. Stravinskas replied.

He explained to his startled friends that the university students and other young people he was encountering were not driven by the anger that characterized the youth of the sixties, or by the rejection of the Church dominant in the seventies. Not that today's students had a robust commitment to the Church, he said, "but they are curious and at times intrigued by the Catholic faith."

"What is lacking in this Catholic restoration?" the editors asked. "There is no vehicle for it," Fr. Stravinskas replied. "We need a new publication that teaches Catholic truth in a mode that is both traditional and contemporary."

Editor Bob Lockwood did not forget that conversation. A year later, upon becoming publisher of *Our Sunday Visitor*, he called Fr. Stravinskas to recruit him as the editor for the publication he had described. "I'm too busy!" the priest objected truthfully. He was teaching full time at a university, had recently been appointed pastor of a church, and was the secretary of a Lithuanian bishop. But Fr. Stravinskas promised to consider the offer and ask a few people for their opinion. To his dismay, no one (including the bishop) had any negative reactions.

So Fr. Stravinskas walked through the door of opportunity which his 1985 comment had opened. The monthly magazine he started, *The Catholic Answer*, has grown remarkably—from 20,000 subscribers to 80,000.

The magazine's format and content have evolved over time, in an ongoing effort to fill the gap that Fr. Stravinskas had perceived. Today one third of each issue is devoted to answering readers' questions about Catholic doctrine, moral teaching, and liturgical practices. (These question and answer columns are collected, indexed by topic, and published as books every three years.) The second third of the magazine is devoted to a particular theme, for example, Catholic history, archaeology, psychology, and the scriptural basis for praying for the dead. One series on the first seven ecumenical councils of the Church showed the way "back into Vatican II" by pointing out the commonality among all councils and their relationship to Vatican II. The last third of *The Catholic Answer* contains general interest articles, like biographies of converts, or the history and background of particular feasts.

Fr. Stravinskas has found his work with the magazine to be enjoyable and not as burdensome as he first thought. In addition, he is finding his initial thesis to be correct: young people are ready for a Catholic restoration. Most of the authors are young, enthusiastic Catholics who love defending and explaining the faith. Not only is their work effective in the present but it is preparing them for a lifetime commitment to the Catholic apostolate.

Fr. Stravinskas walked through an open door to set up a new Catholic magazine, and many other people have followed. This will have a great effect on the future of the Catholic Church in this country.[87]

THE GOSPEL TO THE WHOLE WORLD
—ON TV AND RADIO

Many are the people who bemoan the mental, moral, and spiritual wasteland on television, but few are those who offer alternatives. Mother M. Angelica is among those few.

In 1981 this cloistered Franciscan nun with no previous media background launched the Eternal Word Television Network (EWTN) in response to a local broadcaster's willingness to air a blasphemous program about Jesus Christ. As of August 1995, her courageous move through many open doors is having international impact, with EWTN broadcasting in North and South America, Europe, and Africa. Its sister station, WEWN, a short-wave radio network, reaches around the world to offer multilingual programs. EWTN even has a home page on the World Wide

Web. Mother Angelica's goal is to bring Catholic programming to the whole world.

The basis of EWTN's success is God our Lord. Mother Angelica and her Sisters at Our Lady of the Angels Monastery spend more hours praying before the Blessed Sacrament than they do before the television camera or screen. They maintain that prayerful adoration, meditation, and listening to the Lord address their hearts is the most important element of their broadcasting success; it is God's work, not theirs. As Mother Angelica frequently reminds everyone (and herself, I think), she did not even know how to adjust the color on a television set when she started her network. Her weakness is proof of God's strength.

Obviously EWTN is a tremendous ministry that requires both a large staff and millions of dollars to operate. Most individuals cannot mount such a project no matter how much they may desire good Catholic programming. What ordinary Catholics *can* do, however, is join forces with EWTN and take action to bring the network into their area. Many individuals and organizations like the Knights of Columbus have started petitions to get EWTN included in their local cable schedule.

Chad and Sue Ekberg, a couple from Gillette, Wyoming, made several unsuccessful attempts to get their local cable company to include EWTN. Then one morning early in 1995, while Chad was praying the third glorious mystery of the rosary, he thought of Don Lefevre, of Rapid City, South Dakota, who had gotten EWTN on a local VHF station. Chad approached the owner of a radio tower and the district manager of a VHF station. They offered him a year's worth of air time for $5,000—which is not much money unless you do not have it. But Chad's spiritual advisor encouraged him that "if this project is God's will, he will provide the money." Things moved fast after that. Chad and Sue contacted other Catholics in the area, and with help from them and the network, EWTN went on the air in Gillette on February 14, 1995. Bishop St. Valentine would be proud!

Don Lefevre, whose example inspired Chad, was an electrical engineer involved in television. He asked a friend's father, who owned a low power UHF station, to rent time for EWTN. With help from a priest friend belonging to the Missionaries of the Eternal Word, the new order started at EWTN, Don got EWTN's permission to broadcast the network's signal on UHF. The local stations rented time, the priest blessed the transmitter, Don turned the dish to the EWTN satellite, and the network went on the air.

Don began to wonder: "How many other times has God arranged situations where all that was left was for me to say yes?" Perhaps this is why he was immediately alert when, in November 1995, a business associate told him about a failed South African cable company that would have to broadcast only a test pattern. Through Don's intervention, EWTN broadcasts have replaced the test pattern at no charge, bringing Catholic programming to South Africa.

Don is now convinced that if anyone does what God wants them to do, he will arrange the pieces to make it possible to proclaim the gospel. Other people around the world are discovering this too, as they take similar initiatives—the man in Lake Tahoe, for example, who is building a complete radio station so that EWTN will be available on every local radio. How different the world would be if every Catholic said yes to God, as the Blessed Mother did. If we take the opportunities open before us, God our Lord can use television and radio to proclaim the Good News.[88]

PRESENTATION MINISTRIES: MANY WORKERS FOR GOD'S VINEYARD

Another outreach with which many lay Catholics have joined forces began in the 1970s when a young priest, Fr. Al Lauer, was assigned to the inner-city Church of the Presentation in Cincinnati, Ohio. Not many people came to that church, so Fr. Lauer decided to bring the Catholic Church to the people. He began with door-to-door evangelization, street preaching, and revival meetings, in addition to Sunday Mass. These doors opened wide, with a lot of people finding Jesus Christ, getting baptized, and attending Mass.

Many of these people had been like the unhired laborers in Jesus' parable: just standing around the marketplace until the Master of the vineyard called them. They accepted the summons to work for the Lord with active involvement in the life of the Church. In fact, they started so many ministries, small prayer groups, and faith communities that in 1983 they formed an independent corporation called Presentation Ministries. In the early 1990s they were large enough to become an association of the laity, like the Legion of Mary, Society of St. Paul, or Third Orders of the

Benedictines, Franciscans, Dominicans, and Carmelites.[89]

Today Presentation Ministries includes twenty-three small communities of lay people around the country: ten in Cincinnati, five in Grand Rapids, Michigan, and eight spread throughout the Midwest and central South. These communities pray and work together in support of the association's apostolic activities. Each member of the communities makes a one-year commitment on the feast of Presentation of Jesus in the Temple, February 2, to remain united in prayer and ministry.

These communities support thirty-four ministries of the Word of God, all of which are located in Cincinnati. They include a Bible institute, a discipleship program, and a monthly magazine called *One Bread, One Body*. This publication is translated into Spanish, Indonesian, and Swahili, and is printed in Ghana, Uganda, the Philippines, Myanmar (Burma), Indonesia, and Belize. In the United States alone, over 90,000 copies are printed, though the actual readership is unknown. The magazine is even on the Internet, thanks to the work of one woman, Wallace Mayo, a computer professor at the University of Tennessee.

Presentation Ministries also sponsors a Christian paper called *My People*, with a circulation of ten thousand. They publish twenty thousand copies of a bulletin insert called *John Paul Speaks*, which aims to get papal teaching on a particular topic into Catholic parishes (a surprisingly challenging task). Further support for these works comes from Presentation's third class mailing ministry and UPS ministry, both of which are giant undertakings.

Helping Catholics to read and understand the Bible is

the main goal underlying Presentation Ministries. Fr. Lauer strongly encourages people to attend daily Mass and pay attention to the readings so that they can learn the sacred Scriptures well and find spiritual nourishment in them.

Accordingly, the magazine *One Bread, One Body* focuses on teaching the meaning of the readings for the day's Eucharistic liturgy. So does a twenty-five minute radio program on the Mass readings called "Daily Bread," which has aired Monday through Friday in three cities since 1983. The Bible Telephone Line also presents a message on the daily readings. Fr. Lauer puts the teaching on his phone answering machine each morning, and then people around the country call in to transfer it to an answering machine that makes it available to others in their area.

In a special effort to serve lay people who want to exercise some ministry in the Church, Fr. Lauer is also starting the first Catholic Bible college—Our Lady of Guadalupe Bible College. Most dioceses provide at least some training for church professionals, like directors of religious education. Fr. Lauer wants to reach not only these people but also the majority of Catholics who desire ministry but cannot pursue training full time.

To meet the needs of these lay workers, the Bible college will offer a program that is equivalent to a two-year college degree, available to part-time students in Cincinnati, or as a correspondence course with occasional visits to the college. Since these lay ministers of the future can study only in the context of their everyday life of working and raising children, the college adapts by offering correspondence courses and summer programs that include units for children, from toddlers to teens.

Through Fr. Lauer's creative responses to God-given doors of opportunity, many lay leaders are being discipled and encouraged to proclaim the word of God themselves. Every member of the Church, without exception, is called to this ministry, as Pope John Paul II made clear in his encyclical, *Christifideles Laici* ("The Lay Members of Christ's Faithful People"). Fr. Lauer's own faithfulness to that summons has empowered many lay people who were simply hanging around the marketplace without a sense of Christ's call to serve in his vineyard. Now they too can walk through whatever open doors God sets before them.

OPEN DOORS AHEAD!

These are just a few of the many Catholics who have walked through open doors and started tremendous ministries, on local and national levels. However frustrated they may have felt at the unmet needs or unaddressed errors they noticed, these people took positive steps which have improved life in the Church for all of us.

Not that they have gone from one success to another. But through the inescapable setbacks, problems, and even tragedies of life, they have worked on with hope that God will fulfill his promises. They are confident God's grace will help them through the difficulties, and they possess a faith that works itself out in love (see Gal 5:6).

These creative Catholics stand as examples for us as we too seek to let our frustrations be a catalyst for making a positive contribution to the life of the Church. Admittedly, not all of us are in a position to launch a nationwide organization or to break into the media. But maybe we can participate in the work of ministries that others have founded. Or maybe we can attempt similar initiatives to meet needs on a smaller scale: a local newsletter, for example, or a chat group on the Internet. And even if our talents lie in totally different areas, the creativity of our fellow Catholics can inspire us to put our own special talents fully at God's disposal.

One thing is sure: there is no lack of work in God's vineyard! If we have the desire to serve God and his people, all that remains is to be alert to the doors that God opens before us and to seize each opportunity to walk through.

SEVEN

Do What You Can

Five barley loaves. Two fish. "What good are these for so many?" the apostle Andrew wanted to know, looking at the large and hungry crowd that had followed Jesus (see Jn 6:9). And what were Andrew's thoughts as he helped to gather the leftovers from the five loaves—twelve baskets full, more than the crowd of thousands could eat?

Don't we often react like Andrew when we encounter difficulties and challenging situations in our life as Catholics?

"I'm just an ordinary person. What can *I* do?"

"Maybe this problem will go away if I ignore it."

"Let somebody else take care of it."

Jesus was no ordinary person. Multiplying food is no ordinary response to a problem. Still, Jesus' example teaches us something about what *God* can do when we tackle our problems by working with what we have and doing what we can. Namely, we can take some action and offer

God our efforts—our few loaves and fish—for him to use in the large and small situations that frustrate us. While each of us must decide how best to do this, given our own specific style and problems, a few general guidelines may be helpful.

ORDINARY MEANS

Some frustrated Catholics are like the man whose house was surrounded by rising flood waters. When a rowboat came to evacuate him he said, "No thanks, I'm waiting for the Lord to save me." When a motorboat came to get him from the second-floor window, he repeated his belief. A rescue helicopter hovered over the man as he clung to his roof, but he refused assistance and stuck to his little creed.

The man finally drowned and went to heaven. Seeing the Lord, he demanded an explanation: "Lord, I prayed and prayed. Where were you? Why didn't you save me?"

"Look," the good Lord answered, "I sent you the rowboat, the motorboat, and the helicopter. What were you waiting for?"

Too many frustrated Catholics are like this drowning man—slow to act, slow to recognize the means through which God is providing a way out of frustration. Is it, perhaps, that we are too passive, expecting that God will do something of biblical proportions while we sit back and watch? Is it that we fail to see the Lord's presence in the everyday?

God is with us in our difficulties, even when he does not

reveal himself in miraculous ways—like parting the Red Sea (see Ex 13-14) and causing a large hand to write on the wall (see Dn 5). In fact, it is the ordinary circumstances of life that he uses as the ordinary means to save us. In no way does this limit the Lord to the ordinary, as the miracles of Jesus Christ, his disciples, the saints, and the shrines of Church history amply demonstrate. But generally God acts in the ordinary events and opportunities of life.

Perhaps this suggests that most of us, at least, should reconsider our approach to the everyday. When we look for ways to improve frustrating situations, are we alert to ordinary means and opportunities, or do we await supernatural intervention? Do we take advantage of small openings, or do we put off taking action as we seek some earthshaking strategy?

Years ago, a young woman named Rena opted for the "small and ordinary" approach. She was a new bride at the time, a newcomer in the parish in the small New England town where her husband had grown up. Lonely but also eager to take an active part in parish life, Rena soon discovered that most of the parishioners—including her husband's relatives—mistrusted out-of-staters like her. Furthermore, the pastor exercised rigid control and did not welcome any input from parishioners.

Instead of moping over the lack of outlets for the leadership abilities she had exercised elsewhere, Rena decided to seize ordinary opportunities to do what she could in the parish. She worked on church dinners, fairs, school plays, church-cleaning projects—those behind-the-scenes activities that always need volunteers.

As people got to know and trust Rena, other doors opened: she taught in the religious education program and started a Girl Scout troop within the parish. When the crusty pastor was succeeded by a priest who encouraged lay participation, Rena and her husband became leaders of a parish program that sponsored home discussion groups on topics related to Catholic life. Both were elected to the parish council and served terms as president. Both are Eucharistic ministers.

It took years, but Rena's persistence and attention to ordinary opportunities paid off. Today Rena leads a parish prayer group and serves on a committee to promote family life. But she also helps out with funeral luncheons and the parish thrift shop—still responding to the many ordinary opportunities that are channels for grace and change.

CONFRONT—WITH CHARITY

Fear—whether of failure, controversy, or other people's opinions—blocks many Catholics from doing what they can to address problems in the Church. But as St. Paul wrote to St. Timothy, "God did not give us a spirit of timidity but a spirit of power and love and discipline" (2 Tm 1:7). God the Holy Spirit has not become timid, witless, and obtuse in modern times. Though our own fallen human spirit is weak, causing us to approach problems with timidity or lack of courage and love, the Holy Spirit is all-powerful and active in each Catholic who welcomes him.

Because of this we can be certain that God our Lord will

bestow the power and love necessary to be his instruments of reform and renewal in today's Church. We can face problems squarely, with faith, courage, and confidence. Like St. Paul, we can say with boldness, "I can do all things in him who strengthens me" (Phil 4:13).

Of course, action must not be divorced from wisdom! Before plunging in, we must seek God's help to consider questions such as: Do I have a responsibility to address this problem? What is the most effective approach? Where will I find resources and support? (For some problems, the organizations and reading materials mentioned in this book can provide valuable help.)

In dealing with emotionally charged issues, we must remember the importance of showing charity to all. Too often anger and frustration can result in a grim and loveless approach that promotes bitterness and neglects the main goals of Christ and his Church. This is why we should choose our tactics carefully, while honestly appraising our real motives. Do we want to catch and expose the people we disagree with, or do we want to bring them closer to God? Do we want to get something off our chest, or do we want to make effective changes? Are we simply trying to get our own way, or are we sincerely seeking to contribute to the greater good?

Certainly, it is important to correct abuses, and sometimes public exposure, protests, and other techniques are necessary. But charity dictates that these ought not be the first tactics we use, or the most common.

St. Ignatius of Loyola offers wise advice for confronting such situations. He tells us first of all to give the best possible interpretation to the other person's actions and statements. Assume nothing and get evidence for everything. Gather facts. Avoid guessing at unspoken motives. Do not spread hearsay or rumor: someone else's reputation may be at stake, as well as your own soul, which is damaged by the sins of calumny or slander. Try to speak directly to the persons involved. If they refuse to speak to you, then you may have to involve other people. Do your homework before confronting and before going public, and, if necessary, inform yourself about the Church's teaching on the matter. Perhaps the incident can be more a teaching moment than a scandal.

The way we confront problems large and small in our life in the Church should always be marked by good sense, courtesy, respect, honesty, and an openness to dialogue. These qualities, joined with the courage to address frustrating situations, make us more effective instruments for God. This is not to say that they guarantee success. Sometimes even confronting in charity does not work, and people have to dust off their feet and find a more congenial situation. If this happens to you, just make sure that your being rejected or ignored is because of fidelity to Christ and his Church rather than on account of obnoxious behavior.

FLEXIBLE AND CREATIVE

Jan stalked out of the parish secretary's office in angry frustration. Just a few months before, Jan had been assured that her five-year-old son was "definitely" on the list of children being admitted into the kindergarten class of the parish school. But now on this mid-August morning, Jan was told that her son's name had been dropped. "There's not enough room for all the applicants," the secretary explained. "We have to give priority to parishioners."

"But we *are* parishioners!" Jan exclaimed. "We've been attending this parish for almost two years."

"We have no record of that." The secretary was polite but adamant. Jan and her husband had never bothered to put their Sunday offerings in the collection envelopes issued by the parish. Unfortunately in this parish, receiving and using the envelopes was the only official record of membership.

That evening Jan and her husband discussed their options. Their main goal, they agreed, was to provide their children with a solid Catholic education. Enrolling them in the parochial school was a logical step in that direction. But perhaps there were other ways to realize the same goal.

After some brainstorming, the couple came up with a plan of action. First, they would make more inquiries—just to make absolutely sure that there was no possibility of getting their son into the school this year. They would sign him up for next year's first grade class (and start using the collection envelopes). Next, they would check out some of the other Catholic schools in the area. If all else failed, Jan would consider the option of home-schooling—not a prospect she relished, with two other pre-schoolers to care for.

But all else did fail, and Jan did indeed home-school her son. Things fell into place more easily than she expected, though. She made contact with a local network of home-schooling Catholics and, through them, found solid teaching material and support. Now, excited about home-schooling as a way to help ground her children in their faith, Jan is planning to continue—"at least for a few more years."

Like Jan and her husband, all of us encounter obstacles as we try to realize our goals. How should we respond?

I suggest that we praise God for these disappointments, which can motivate us to deal with problems we would otherwise leave unresolved. If we have tried an approach and failed, we can praise God for finding out what did not work. Failures are learning experiences by which we eliminate ineffective strategies. Failures challenge us to become even more creative and clever in finding better techniques to improve frustrating situations in our life in the Church.

This calls for a certain flexibility, an openness to changing our direction or tactics. While we must never compromise on our basic goals, insofar as they reflect Christ's goals for us and for the Church, we must develop the ability to consider other possible means to the same end.

The Holy Spirit will guide us in this, helping us to maintain a balance between being either too rigid or too easily swayed on the essentials. In matters great and small, we can always trust this best Counselor of all to inspire and encourage, to show us a way to do what we can.

PRESERVE UNITY

Leaders of a parish prayer group, upset that Pastor X seems to be neglecting them, refuse to support the Bible study he is launching. Mrs. Y declines to make her usual contribution of hand-knit items to sell at the parish bazaar: she is miffed at not being asked to serve as a Eucharistic minister. Mr. Z, frustrated over certain Church teachings he does not understand, stops making his annual contribution to the diocesan services appeal.

What has happened to the unity Jesus prayed for at the Last Supper: "that they may all be one, as you, Father, are in me and I in you" (Jn 17:21)? How easily we forget this goal of Christ's when we are caught up in the heat of emotion or are pursuing our own misguided solution to a problem. And yet how crucial it is to work for improvements in a way that promotes unity within the body of Christ.

For this to happen, we Catholics must realize that we are all on the same team and should be striving together for the basic goals which Christ set for the Church. The goal is not the defeat of any particular wing or group or individual, but the conversion of everyone to a deeply committed love of Christ and his Church. The goal is not to get back at any organization but to win everyone over to believe the gospel. The goal is not for the triumph of any one particular style of worship but for a truly Catholic celebration of the holy sacrifice of the Mass. And so on.

One area where unity is especially needed and would be especially fruitful concerns the relationships among various conservative reform movements in the Church. Some of these—like the Cursillo movement and two of its offshoots, the charismatic renewal and Marriage Encounter—are more emotionally expressive. So are some of the Marian movements driven by reported visions and inner locutions in the 1980s and 1990s. Other groups—among them, Opus Dei, Catholics United for the Faith, and Latin Mass proponents—push forward reform with a more theological emphasis. Obviously these groups have different styles of praying and communicating, usually identified by in-group vocabulary and interests.

Unfortunately, such groups tend to be unable to get along with each other, let alone cooperate to promote church renewal and reform. Some conservatives will not come near a charismatic gathering for fear of having to hug complete strangers or sing choruses with a lively beat. They wonder in frustration where the solemn dignity of Gregorian chant and the Latin Mass have gone. Charismatics exuberantly invite everyone to come to their Masses and meetings in order to get free of stuffiness and rigidity. Proponents of the Fatima apparitions are appalled at the new and currently unapproved visions at Medjugorje and other places. Some do not accept the validity of the Pope's consecration of the world to the Blessed Virgin Mary; others do.

How much richer the Church would be if all of these groups learned to respect each other and work together while preserving their own appropriate character. There is room for great diversity and freedom in the Church so long as the one, holy, Catholic faith that comes from the apostles is maintained. Each group has important elements to contribute to Church renewal.

When churches that look like malls, theaters, and gymnasia are decorated by art that seems inspired by the Jetsons' or Flintstones' decor, the Catholic community needs the sensitivities of people who love Michelangelo and Giotto and icons to help design the churches. When the music switches from folk styles to pop, and the lyrics praise the congregation instead of the Lord, the haunting beauties of Gregorian chant would be preferred.[90]

On the other side, when the desire for a meditative atmosphere in a church turns into a cool indifference among parishioners, the affectionate caring of a charismatic group—its willingness to pray for the sick and help the emotionally bruised—is a great gift. The Marian movement is wonderful for its boldness in motivating parishioners to pray the rosary after daily Mass, start Marian prayer groups, adore the Blessed Sacrament, and go on pilgrimages.

In addition, many groups sponsor seminars, workshops, and conferences on topics of mutual interest to other groups. Even if rumors suggest that a conference is going to use Latin chant at their Masses, the charismatics can attend and learn more about pro-life issues or some deeper theology of the sacraments. Even if a charismatic conference has a lot of people raising their hands and swaying to the beat of a hymn, the Latin Mass Society members can let go a little and learn about evangelization or other important topics.

Beyond mutual attendance at each other's functions,

these renewal movements can develop respect for each other and begin to network effectively. How can Marriage Encounter help the pro-life groups? Where can the Latin Mass Society serve the local Marian conference or provide musical assistance? The leaders of these various movements should seek each other out, explore areas of possible cooperation, and make explicit efforts to pray for one another.

The call to unity is addressed to all of us, of course, not only to leaders and members of renewal groups. Make it a priority as you work to change your particular frustrating situation. Set competition aside. Seek solutions that are not divisive. Reach out. Try to reason together. Try to work together with your fellow Catholics, insofar as possible. The whole Church will benefit.

A SPIRIT OF SERVICE

Looking for ways to be of service is part of our call to imitate Jesus, who said, "I am among you as the one who serves" (Lk 22:27). It is also a great way to deal with frustration—especially in those areas of the Church where we see needs, opportunities, and matters for concern.

This spirit of service characterizes the people whose stories appear in the rest of this chapter. These are Catholics who have recognized an opportunity and taken the initiative to do what they could. Their "loaves and fish" have not turned into national ministries or organizations, but they are providing much-needed nourishment nonetheless.

Matt Pinto, a Philadelphia salesman in his early twenties, had some new doors open for him after he joined the St. Matthias Sunday night young adults' group. The three other young adults who organized and led the group showed Matt a dynamic way to be Catholic, and opened his eyes to the wisdom of the Church. Twenty-three-year-old Michael Wallacavage, a graduate of Christendom College who was radically on fire for his faith, made a special impression. His example engendered in Matt the same fire in mind, heart, and will to become a godly man.

Under Michael's leadership, the young adults' group evolved into a Bible study. As Matt learned more about Catholicism, he acquired a taste for apologetics. This led him to the 1989 "Defending the Faith" conference in Steubenville, where Matt heard Karl Keating, founder of Catholic Answers, deliver a lecture (see chapter 6). Deciding to put his marketing skills to work for the gospel, Matt invited Karl to hold an apologetics lecture in Philadelphia. This bold move was a tremendous success, with a large audience attending the lecture. Matt's effective promotional work also resulted in two very successful formal debates between Catholic Answers and some anti-Catholics; five hundred people attended each one.

Six months after the second lecture, Matt was presented with a more radical opportunity to serve: Karl Keating invited him to do the marketing work for Catholic Answers. Matt responded like the first disciples on the Sea of Galilee, who left their nets to follow Jesus. He sold his flourishing advertising and marketing business and moved to San Diego in March 1991 to take up his new service.

Seeking even more outlets for service, Matt approached the pastor of centrally located old Mission San Diego church and presented him with a well-organized proposal for a young adults' group. With the pastor's approval, Matt set to work. One weekend he and some friends passed out promotional flyers in the mission church, and after every Mass he gave a three-minute pitch on why young adults need a Catholic faith group as an alternative to night clubs and fitness centers as a place to meet, socialize, and learn. In response, thirty young adults came to the group's first meeting on November 11, 1991.

Today sixty to seventy young people attend the meetings every Wednesday night, enjoying refreshments and socializing, lectures by outside speakers, videotapes, and talks and discussions on Scripture, Catholic doctrine, and morals. The group sponsors a monthly Holy Hour and also collects money for the poor and clothes for a crisis pregnancy center. Once a month it holds a peaceful, prayerful protest at a local abortion clinic; at pro-life marches it has the largest turnout of any San Diego group. Many members evangelize nominal or fallen-away Catholics. In addition to all this activity, one member has joined a contemplative religious order, and a few marriages have developed within the group, including Matt's.

Amazing what can happen when a Catholic gets on fire for God.

Margaret Setyko began to commit herself more seriously to service in the Church after making a series of pilgrimages. After reading a newspaper report about apparitions of the Blessed Virgin Mary in Yugoslavia, Margaret signed up for a 1984 pilgrimage to Medjugorje, becoming one of the first Americans to visit St. James Church there. The Communists' refusal to allow the pilgrims to stay more than one day only whetted Margaret's appetite for pilgrimage: she returned six months later and stayed with a villager for a few days.

Motivated to study more about visionaries and saints, Margaret went on more pilgrimages—to Italy, Fatima, and Lourdes, as well as Medjugorje. In June 1988 Margaret and her husband went to Medjugorje with their four children, who were not merely reticent but belligerent about making a pilgrimage. However, after spending a little time there, they experienced a conversion and enthusiastically joined in the prayer, rosaries, Masses, and confession. The family's conversion continued to deepen through other trips, and Margaret even experienced a healing of breast cancer on a pilgrimage.

Personal conversion led Margaret to a desire for service in the most normal place of all—her own parish. She began by starting a prayer group, meeting every month after the parish's regular Tuesday night Mass. The first night one hundred and fifty people showed up for Mass and stayed on for the rosary. Margaret added a little evangelization to the meeting and made available religious books, leaflets, and videos about the Bible and lives of the saints.

Margaret discovered that Catholics are hungry to know more about their faith. In response, she has sold thousands of dollars worth of books, mostly at cost, and arranged for outside speakers to address the prayer group. Other parishioners have joined in to help as the group has expanded; for instance, twelve couples have organized to develop and lead a weekly outreach for children in the parish.

In May 1995 Margaret and her husband started another apostolate of prayer when they asked their pastor to allow weekly exposition and adoration of Christ in the Blessed Sacrament. This now happens every Friday from 8:30 A.M. to 8:30 P.M., with Margaret and her husband overseeing the effort. During the week they set out charts and ask people to sign up for an hour of prayer at a specific time. On Friday they are present in the morning when adoration starts, and in the evening when it ends.

Awakened by pilgrimages, Margaret's spirit of service to the Church is benefiting many people, drawing them in turn to do what they can.

Fr. Daniel Johnson, pastor of St. Mary by the Sea parish in Huntington Beach, California, looks for ways to serve even on his weekly day off. Every Wednesday finds him doing door-to-door evangelism in the neighborhood.

Fr. Johnson is a soft-spoken man who uses a soft-sell approach in keeping with his personality. If someone answers the door, he asks if there are any Catholics in the house who need to be baptized, confirmed, or go to confession. He invites them to church, leaves his card, and with a smile walks on to the next door. If no one answers, he leaves his card and moves on.

Fr. Johnson finds that people willingly accept his visits—something he attributes to the fact that he always wears his clerical collar, which identifies him as a servant of Jesus

Christ. Whatever the reasons, his approach is successful: Fr. Johnson's congregation has doubled since 1978, when he became pastor of the then-struggling parish. Inactive Catholics and new converts alike join the parish in response to God our Lord working through this friendly outreach in a California beach town. In 1994 alone, forty-five adults became Catholics there.

Like Fr. Johnson, many other Catholics throughout the country are rising to the challenge of door-to-door evangelism, an outreach that typically has been carried out by Mormons and Jehovah's Witnesses. One Chicago parish trains lay people to do surveys door to door. Surveyers come ready both to ask and answer questions about the Church. They also bring a one-page list of all the local churches of every denomination, with addresses, phone numbers, and worship schedules; they give these to people who say they are not Catholic and do not know the location of their church. This act of charity warms the recipient to the Catholic caller and may open doors at a later date.

A parish in San Antonio, Texas, has a team that has visited everyone in the parish. Members see themselves as evangelizers more than surveyors, and they explicitly aim to win people for the faith. Their success has been shown by the growth of thirty prayer groups and Bible studies of different kinds. Mass attendance is up, and people participate very actively in parish functions.

In a wealthy town in Florida, a woman of means surveying the parish discovered that pockets of poor people lived within the parish limits. She and other parishioners began to help them with their faith, their homes, jobs, and families. Their most dramatic experience was when they knocked on the door of a woman who was about to commit suicide. She agreed to visit the parish priest, get counseling, return to confession and the sacraments, and accept help in other areas of her life.

As many Catholics are discovering, door-to-door evangelism is a simple and non-threatening way to spread the gospel and to bridge barriers of isolation. It benefits not only the people contacted but also the evangelizers, who grow in their own faith and commitment to serving God.

Mark Brumley, a layman with a spirit of service, is an example of quiet, professional excellence at work for the Church. Mark began his career of service as a member of the Catholic Answers staff. Then, asked to work for the diocese of San Diego, he set up a social ministries office and later became director of diocesan communications. In 1993 Mark was named assistant publisher of *Southern Cross,* the diocesan newspaper, which was then fighting to hold its own against a free, privately published competitor that specialized in reports of abuses and problems in the diocese.

Concerned about abuses but also about publications that focus on problems in the Church without providing positive teaching, Mark began to revamp the *Southern Cross* to make it more readable and more explicitly evangelistic. His first goal was to clearly proclaim the gospel and invite readers to accept Jesus' offer of salvation. The content of the paper now reflects this purpose. So does a new public distribution program that aims to reach the secular world: through it the *Southern Cross* is sent to libraries, coffee shops, restaurants, and prisons in the area.

The results of Mark's creative and diligent efforts: in 1994 circulation increased by 25 percent, and the *Southern Cross* received an award for general excellence from the Catholic Communications Campaign. Not so easy to measure is the newspaper's undeniable spiritual impact on readers, who are but the latest beneficiaries of Mark's desire to serve and his step-by-step response to opportunities big and small.

Many, many more Catholics could be mentioned here as examples of people who are doing what they can to improve some situation in the Church.

I think of Fr. John Phillips, of St. John Cantius Parish, in Chicago. He used to feel hopeless and frustrated about the spread of liturgical abuses in the Church. Then he realized that he could at least work to make his own parish liturgies as beautiful and God-centered as possible. The result is truly majestic worship whose high point is the Sunday morning Latin Mass sung with Gregorian chant. And because the beauty of the Catholic liturgy attracts people, the congregation, located in a depopulated inner city area, has grown steadily; many young families and young adults now attend, as well as older people, and a spirit of community is developing.

I think of Fr. John O'Holohan, S.J., who after years of teaching and spiritual direction, mostly in Africa, began a new service in parish ministry in Florida. He has devised a way to present the Spiritual Exercises of St. Ignatius of Loyola, normally a thirty-day retreat, to busy lay people—

seventy-three in the last six years. The program is flexible but rigorous, requiring much prayer, reading, spiritual direction, and follow-up. Retreatants come away from the experience with a new hunger for God and detachment from things like money, ambition, power. They also have a renewed desire to serve, which benefits others in the Church. At the parish where Fr. O'Holohan is stationed, for instance, four retreatants and another friend started a movement to institute perpetual adoration of the Blessed Sacrament: eight hundred people signed up to pray for an hour every week.

There is Chris, a North Carolina businessman who has been concerned that so few men are active in the parish. With his pastor's encouragement, he organized a network of small groups to provide fellowship and support for building family and parish life. About thirty men now take part in these weekly meetings.

There is Linda, a single woman whose journey out of deep depression began when she made a commitment to attend daily Mass. Now, through her behind-the-scenes counsel, prayer, and organizing of events that foster faith, Linda helps others in her Michigan parish to move towards the deeper relationship with God that she has discovered.

All across the country, in quiet ways and in more obvious ones, these and so many other Catholics are faithfully offering their little "loaves and fish" to God. Our own challenges and frustrations give us an opportunity to do this, too. With faith and love, then, let us offer our efforts to the One who can multiply them beyond all our hopes.

EIGHT

If This Is the Way You Treat Your Friends...

A famous incident in the life of St. Teresa of Avila entailed an important visit to a bishop in another town. She cleaned and pressed her habit, got in a cart, and was driven to the bishop's see. On the way, the cart hit a bump in a river ford and knocked St. Teresa into the muddy stream. She looked up to heaven and said, "Lord, if this is the way You treat Your friends, it is no wonder that You have so few!" Most people can sympathize with St. Teresa because they have their own negative reaction to suffering and frustration.

Mary teaches at a Catholic college which is sponsoring an event to honor a Catholic politician who has been an outspoken advocate of abortion rights. She speaks up at a faculty planning meeting and registers her disapproval. As Mary had suspected, her protest has no effect—except to identify her as a reactionary and a troublemaker. Now she feels somewhat ostracized. Even her anti-abortion colleagues think that Mary overreacted. "After all," they point out after the event, "the bishop himself never uttered a word of protest."

Rick and Peggy have tried for years to communicate their concerns about gambling to their pastor and the parish council. Weekly bingo games, endless raffles, regular trips to local casinos organized by the senior citizens' group, an array of lotteries and games of chance at the parish's annual fair—these activities are too prominent in their parish, they feel. "But they're our biggest source of revenue," retorts the parish finance committee. And so Rick and Peggy watch on as the gambling addiction that is sweeping the country gets a deeper hold on many of their fellow parishioners.

Representatives from area churches are meeting to plan a fundraising event to benefit the homeless. When Julie volunteers to attend as her parish's delegate, she discovers that the parish never participates in either ecumenical ventures or social action projects. Attempts to persuade parish leaders are fruitless. "We just don't do that kind of thing," Julie is firmly informed.

NOT JUST A BOWL OF CHERRIES

None of us is guaranteed success in our attempts to change frustrating situations and contribute to Church renewal. Sometimes our goals are not very good.

Sometimes we have not really thought things through or chosen a realistic plan of action. Our sinfulness and personality weaknesses can keep us from being effective. Other people's sin and personality problems get in the way. And even with the best goals, strategies, and efforts, we can certainly expect to meet with at least occasional failure and rejection.

How can we learn to cope with the pain and difficulty of defeat? How do we react to the negativity and opposition of fellow members of the body of Christ? How can we grow through the experiences of failure that accompany the service of Jesus Christ and his Church?

Though there is much we cannot know about suffering, we can have every confidence that God will turn it to our good. This confidence will grow stronger as we learn to put aside some of our misguided explanations about why we have failed.

"I didn't have enough faith." It is not helpful to expect success and blessing at every turn. Certainly, it is never wrong to ask God our Lord for an increase in faith or to seek a greater trust in God. This should never be seen as insurance against failure, however. God does not always bring success to the Christian who simply believes hard enough.

One could hardly accuse our Lord Jesus Christ of a lack of faith, yet he experienced notable setbacks: opposition from the leadership of various religious parties, misunderstanding by family and friends, betrayal and abandonment by his disciples in his moment of greatest need, shameful torture and execution by the Roman government. Could we possibly stand with Christ in Gethsemane and say, "Just ask for a little more faith, Jesus, and you will be blessed out of your socks!"? Neither should we superficially summon our struggling brothers and sisters—or ourselves—with a call to faith that is nothing but a hidden accusation of a lack of faith.

On the other hand, neither should we discourage others—or ourselves—from seeking "faith the size of a mustard seed" so as to move sycamore trees into the sea (see Lk 17:6). Each of us needs the Holy Spirit's gift of faith (see 1 Cor 12:9) so that the Lord can use us to accomplish his mighty deeds. Throughout sacred Scripture God makes tremendous promises to help and protect anyone who trusts in him. Reading through the Bible to find these promises and asking for an increased faith to believe them can yield great benefits. However, such faith does not preclude the possibility of suffering and pain in the lives of believers. Read the Scriptures and the lives of the saints to see how God's chosen ones suffer much for the sake of the kingdom of God.

"It's all *their* fault." Another hazardous response to failure and pain is the search to assign the blame to others. We human beings are notoriously reluctant to admit and take responsibility for our sins and faults and to repent of them. Remember how Adam and Eve deflected their blame? This is why a regular examination of conscience is so important (see chapter three).

Most of us, at least sometimes, point the finger at

someone or something else in order to avoid taking personal responsibility for failure. Commonly this is an expression of anger and a desire (at least implicit) to get back at someone who has offended us or obstructed our plans. Blaming is a way to retaliate, to harm our offenders verbally, psychologically, physically, or through the mental gymnastics of imagining the delight of vengeance.

Blaming is an unhealthy, unproductive response to pain and failure that usually does more harm to the one assigning the blame than to the intended target.

"I just knew it would never work." Despair, which is the loss of hope for improvement, is another false approach to crises and failures. Often, we use statements of hopelessness as attempts to justify ourselves and remove personal blame for failure.

Despair also justifies our decision to give up working for renewal or reform, or even to stop trying to address our frustrations; it permits us to return to personal pursuits and an unsatisfactory status quo, rather than seek the good of the Church and the greater glory of God.

Such despair fails to detect any benefit in pain and closes off the possibility of growing from it. Hope in God and faith in his infinite love for each person, no matter what the circumstances, is the start for making spiritual progress through suffering. It is the road to becoming stronger Christians, as well as dealing with difficulties and making a contribution to the Church.

Setbacks and problems, pain and suffering are inevitable in life, and therefore in our experience of life in the Church.

But instead of treating these experiences as failures, we should see them for what they are: opportunities for growth and development.

Sometimes suffering stimulates us to find more creative solutions to problems. Sometimes it must simply be endured. Especially in the latter case—when we may or may not perceive, even dimly, the positive future outcome to which our suffering is leading—we will be able to endure it with greater hope if we have some understanding of God's creative plan for suffering.

SUFFERING AS DISCIPLINE

Pain teaches us that certain limits exist beyond which we may not safely pass. How many adolescents refuse to believe that there can be too much booze or too little sleep? Many adults have trouble accepting the fact that one can eat too many fat grams or receive too little exercise. As a boy, I did not believe that there could ever be too much Halloween candy, too much ice cream or cake.

Sometimes when my personal failure to observe life's limits came to my father's attention, he carefully considered the use of his belt to refocus my attention. My refusals to live within the limits imposed by nature or the rights of other persons would induce Dad to underscore his message with a bit of red highlighter across my bottom. This had a salutary effect which I came to appreciate better in retrospect than at the moment.

God's fatherly love also includes a willingness to discipline us, as Scripture points out.

> My son, do not despise the Lord's discipline
>   or be weary of his reproof,
> For the Lord reproves him whom he loves,
>   as a father the son in whom he delights.
>
> PROVERBS 3:11-12

The New Testament frequently cites this passage. The letter to the Hebrews, for example, quotes it in the context of helping the early Christians to understand the persecution they were suffering (see Heb 12:5-6). The letter goes on to state that illegitimate children lose out by not having the discipline of dads who care enough about the outcome of their lives to tell them "No" when necessary. Good fathers use various forms of discipline to correct children who insist on foolish or mischievous behavior. Likewise, God our Father disciplines his children "for a short time... for their own good, that they may share in his holiness" and the "peaceful fruit of righteousness" (Heb 12:10-11).

Of course, the immediate experience of God's discipline is not pleasant. But the pain of discipline is not meant to be enjoyed but learned from. Therefore, the task is to reflect on painful situations and see if there is some lesson to learn.

LESSONS FROM THE CLASSROOM

Two of the more notable occasions in which I learned about God's discipline were assignments by my superiors to teach high school religion. When I undertook this in 1972, I had little understanding of teaching techniques and disdained as backwards anything that struck me as being regimented and authoritarian.

"High school students should be trusted to take responsibility for learning," I used to rant. "Why embarrass them with tests or quizzes?" Treat these young people as adults, and you will spontaneously evoke their respect for the teacher, fellow students, and the learning process, was my theory. Was I wrong! The freshmen had more control of the class than I did. I could not understand why being a nice guy would not make the students into nice guys.

In addition to being a poor disciplinarian, I did not have a good grasp of what I should be teaching. At that point I was still fascinated with the enneagram, yoga, astrology, and other New Age practices. I assumed that my students would love to learn the deeply meaningful (not to mention groovy) yogic meditations. Of course, they considered these techniques worthy only of their ridicule, inside and outside of class. Teaching high school was an awful experience, but through its miseries I learned a number of important lessons.

First, obedience is important. Religious life as a Jesuit is not characterized by doing my own thing but by serving the greater glory of God as a member of the Society of Jesus. The vow of obedience I have taken means that I am not free to do whatever I want, whenever I think it most opportune, in order to do whatever seems most fulfilling.

Vow of obedience or not, part of everyone's maturing process is learning that our egos are not the hub of the universe and the world does not turn only to meet our needs. Discipline, tough as it is, wakes us up to the cold hard fact that everybody has to learn how to fit into a much larger world containing other people with legitimate needs and wants.

Working for Church renewal, or even dealing with petty frustrations in our life in the Church, necessarily entails belonging to the larger community of the Church and learning to work with the legitimate demands of fellow Christians. Sometimes this means obeying lawful church authorities when personal opinion would take us in other directions. Following an order or direction that contradicts what we believe to be right, more intelligent, or more effective, is most difficult. Yet everyone must obey legitimate authorities (excepting, of course, when ordered to commit sin).

Our Lord Jesus Christ himself learned obedience through what he suffered. Read the first seventeen chapters of John's Gospel carefully, and you will see that each one contains a statement by Christ that he came not to do his own will but the will of his Father. Archbishop Sheen frequently pointed out that Christ spent thirty years obeying, three years teaching, and three hours redeeming. From

Christ Jesus' own example all Christians are to learn the discipline of obedience, trusting that God will use their acts of obedience for his greater glory.

Second, failure sometimes paves the way for success. From the misery of teaching high school, I learned that *failures stimulate us to learn*. Precisely because the teenagers were a difficult audience, I became a better communicator. College students, who have become inculturated to a higher tolerance for boredom, would not have called as much effort from me. I am forever grateful that fidgety boys motivated me to develop the teaching skills that I possess. The desolate experience of being forced to teach high school students taught me how to outline my ideas, get my facts straight, and field questions.

Of course, I did not understand any of this at the time. The lessons learned through failure are not always immediate or apparent. But if we probe our difficult experiences, rejections, and frustrations, we can often grasp their purpose—especially as we grow in trust that God is working through every circumstance.

St. Paul wrote, "We know that for those who love God everything works out for good for those who are called according to his plan" (Rom 8:28). "Affliction, distress, persecution, hunger, nakedness, danger, and the sword"—according to St. Paul, these are challenges which cannot separate any believer from Christ but which can work out for the good. They are not good things in themselves, but they can work out for God's glory. Elsewhere St. Paul gives similar lists and boasts about his persecution and suffering for the sake of the gospel (see 2 Cor 6 and 12). If St. Paul could find the good in being beaten with rods, stoned nearly to death, and shipwrecked, then surely every Christian can find God's good will and purpose in such lesser trials as teaching high school students!

Third, pain teaches us what *not* to do—in my case, what not to teach. Every Sunday of my first semester of teaching, I would sit in my room and cry because I had no idea what I would do in that week's class. Each Friday I would return to my room to cry again because the week had been so awful. The students' ridicule of the New Age ideas I so dearly espoused showed me that something was wrong. Eventually, when one group of boys got me to be the moderator of a small charismatic prayer group, I discovered what the students *did* want to hear about: sacred Scripture and the Catholic faith.

At this time I was undergoing a personal reconversion, so I eased into the subject of true Christianity by having the boys read books like *The Cross and the Switchblade,* by David Wilkerson, a Pentecostal minister.[91] They enjoyed the exciting stories, and we were all challenged by Wilkerson's faith. Then we read novels and apologetics books by C.S. Lewis, books which made my conversion intellectually possible. In the process I became motivated to investigate more of the riches of the Catholic faith, and I learned some of the theology that still forms the basis of my own beliefs. The triteness and superficiality of the New Age books I had once enjoyed became manifest, as did the depths of Catholic writers like G.K. Chesterton, Cardinal

John Henry Newman, and the saints.

These new intellectual directions have been worth every bit of the anguish caused by my earlier failures in the classroom. By guiding us away from what is harmful, God's discipline points us toward what is good and true.

Fourth, suffering prods us to pray. The crisis in my classroom moved me to pray more and re-examine my commitment to Jesus Christ and the Catholic Church. At times I felt such desolation that all seemed darkness, with our Lord's call to be a Jesuit as the sole pinpoint of light in my life. I sought the Lord in prayer, I begged for help in the classroom, and I pleaded for the Lord to take me out of the high school.

The main result of this prayer was conversion. I moved from seeking a state of spiritual consciousness to desiring a personal relationship with the Triune God—Father, Son, and Holy Spirit. I experienced a deeper repentance for sin, which I now saw as an offense against the personal God rather than an abstract failure. I grew in faith as I sought God's message in the sacred Scriptures rather than in various New Age or pop psychology books. Ever since, I have pursued God's grace, and that conversion has deepened.

A LESSON FROM THE LAODICEAN CHRISTIANS

Frustrated Catholics who let their suffering draw them to God will receive rich blessings. In the book of Revelation's warning to the complacent and lukewarm

Christians of Laodicea, the Lord explains his desire to sell the Laodiceans his gold and make them truly rich, to clothe them in white garments that cover their shame, and to anoint their eyes with his salve that they might see (see Rv 3:14-17). "Those whom I love, I reprove and chasten, so be zealous and repent," he tells the Laodiceans.

The Lord is most willing to shake Christians out of complacency, self-satisfaction, and contentment with the status quo so as to give them something better. We are not merely to endure the pain of discipline and correction but to zealously repent and seek out the greater goods that the Lord offers us.

The best response is to express zeal in repentance by praising and thanking God for the discipline he sends our way. Instead of chafing at the bit, thank God for the bit that makes it possible for him to reprove, chasten, and direct us. This attitude requires great faith, but it also stirs up a more ardent faith. It brings with it peace, serenity, and joy, even in the hardest learning experiences of life.

SUFFERING BEYOND UNDERSTANDING

Much of our pain comes from the ordinary problems and difficulties we encounter. Most of our frustrations in the Church are of this type, and difficult though they may be, it is not impossible to view them as learning opportunities. But sometimes life brings profoundly horrible experiences which generate such radical suffering that they defy meaningful explanation. Deadly disease, crimes of violence, wholesale slaughters like the Nazi destruction of the Jews, Gypsies, and others, or the Communist execution of over sixty million people in the Soviet Union and seventy million in Maoist China—suffering of this type cannot be trivialized by quick explanations.

How, then, are we to understand such disasters? How do we cope with them when they arise in our own life and the lives of those near to us? What benefit can there be to such profoundly distressing situations?

The Book of Job, while not providing answers to these questions, helps us through its portrayal of a man reacting in anguish to a series of horrific disasters piled one on top of another. Job, a Gentile who is righteous in God's sight, loses his children, his vast property, and his health simply because Satan wants to test his righteousness. Though he refuses to "curse God and die," Job still wants to know why he is suffering. His friends offer many suggestions, most of which center on the idea that Job is being punished for some sin. Job maintains his own innocence and repeatedly asks God for an explanation.

Finally, the Lord appears to Job in a whirlwind and asks him to answer a few simple questions about the creation of the world and the mysterious ways it operates (see Jb 38-41). If Job can understand those mysteries, then he can understand why he is suffering. Realizing his ignorance, Job wisely covers his mouth to prevent himself from saying anything more (Jb 40:4-5), and he repents of trying to answer questions beyond his comprehension (Jb 42:1-6). He offers sacrifices for his three friends who, by accusing Job of sin, "had not spoken rightly" of God. The episode ends happily as Job's health, family, and fortunes are restored (42:7-17).

Not everyone endures such dreadfully painful sufferings as Job and so many other people throughout history. Nonetheless, many people undergo personal agonies, and no amount of explanation removes the pain. Nor does commitment to the Lord's work (which has enough problems attached to it) exempt anyone from the experience of personal tragedies. On Sunday, October 10, 1992, I relearned this familiar lesson in a particularly excruciating way.

REMEMBERING MISSY

That day I returned from celebrating Mass to find a message waiting for me: my cousin, Missy, had died. I called her mom and learned the tragic news that two boys had raped and stabbed Missy to death while she was babysitting three infant cousins. Neighbors had heard her screams but paid no attention, and so Missy—just three weeks short of her seventeenth birthday—was murdered.

Missy's mother had already lost her first husband to a murder during a robbery. Her second husband, my cousin Tom, died of cancer at age thirty-six. Now her oldest child had been raped and killed so brutally that the police would not let us see her body.

Like Job's friends, it was tempting to ask, "Why would God do such a thing to her or to any of us who loved Missy?" Of course, I knew, *God* would not do this. How could he whom the angels call thrice holy (see Is 6:3) pro-voke someone to break his own fifth and sixth command-ments? God desires everyone to keep the holy command-ments to protect and sanctify life, not take it. God is not the author of evil; neither does he motivate anyone else to sin in order to punish other sinners. But knowing all of this does not remove the questions. The reasons for Missy's horrible, lonely death and for our family's grief remain mys-teries.

Missy's funeral was, after my mother's funeral, the most difficult I have ever celebrated. I could not explain her suf-fering or our family's. In the homily, the only thing I could do was call my family to renew our Catholic faith in the midst of the pain. The murderers had robbed us of Missy, and we could do nothing about their act. However, if we allowed their crime to take away our faith in God, then they would have robbed us twice, and we would be respon-sible for our loss of faith. Precisely in the face of losing Missy, we needed to deepen our relationship with God. Until the day we see her again, our task is to stay close to God, do what he asks, and get to heaven ourselves.

The pain of Missy's death remains, but God is helping us to move on. The process is unlike those less painful instances of God's discipline that teach a lesson. But some-how, through accepting the mystery of unexplainable agony, we are being invited to grow in wisdom.

Certainly, one element in growing through this degree of pain is learning a new level of forgiveness. My immediate reaction to learning the circumstances of Missy's murder was to want to kill her murderers. Either a vigilante killing by the men of the family or execution by the state would have suited my desires for vengeance just fine. As my shock wore off, I began to pray for Missy's killers, that they would make a good confession and be reconciled to God. I still would have been willing to pull any switch or push any button to execute them after their conviction. Only after time did I learn to put aside my desire for revenge and simply pray for these two young men and for their spiritual conversion. Where no argument from opponents of the death penalty had been able to sway me, I was changed and softened through the Lord's peaceful presence in prayer, the reminders of his forgiveness of my own sins, and time to reflect.

Another dimension of experiencing deep pain is an increased ability to empathize with other afflicted people. In the days when I thought that God would grant me a charmed life free from catastrophes, I could remain aloof from the suffering of others. Perhaps I judged them in a subtle way, thinking that they might have done something to deserve their pain. Certainly, my own shallowness made me incapable of understanding the reality and depth of others' grief. Missy's death and other agonizing experiences have helped me to identify with the pain of other people. Now I can relate to them rather than ignore them until they feel as good as I do. I feel more human as a result.

One last effect of unexplainable suffering in my life has been to deepen my understanding of the psalms of lament. The lament is one of the forms of speech that Scripture scholars have identified in the Book of Psalms. There are hymns of praise or thanksgiving, enthronement psalms, wisdom psalms, and other types. The psalms of lament—most commonly for the individual and the community—comprise about two thirds of the whole psalter. These psalms became the staple of my prayer and meditation throughout another anguishing episode, my parents' separation and divorce.

A TIME TO LAMENT

The shock of my family's breakdown began for me in June 1981. After attending a friend's first Mass, I had driven to my parents' farm to surprise Dad with a Father's Day visit. No one was home, so I assumed they were visiting some friends for a cookout or dinner. When I called our closest family friends to ask if my parents were there, they seemed puzzled. "Have you spoken to your folks recently?" they asked. It had been a few weeks since our last contact.

Our family friend, Ben, drove to our farm to pick me up and tell me that my parents were having some trouble; he also arranged for my parents to come to their house. That was when I learned that Dad had moved in with another woman. Outraged, I slammed my fists down and exploded with anger. Later Ben's wife, Pat, said she had never before seen someone's heart break in front of her.

In that year when my parents divorced each other after thirty-one years of marriage, I felt bitter anguish, anger, and great embarrassment. The divorce felt like an amputation, with my loyalties splitting in two directions. Dad and Mom could no longer enjoy normal family events together, which marred their children's celebrations of life. They would not sit together at my brother's graduation from high school; each refused to attend my doctoral graduation if the other was to be there, and so on. And how could I teach other people about family life when my own family had broken up?

Fortunately, at our diaconate ordination, we priests take a vow to pray the Liturgy of the Hours daily. At the time of my parents' divorce, I focused on the psalms of lament. Not every word or phrase fit my situation, but enough of them did and they became the way I spoke to God in prayer. I sat and meditated on lines such as,

> You made us a taunt to our neighbors, a mockery and-derision to those who surround us.
> You have made us a byword among the nations, a shak-ing of the head to the peoples.
> All day my humiliation is before me, and shame covers my face."   PSALMS 44:14-16

These verses especially struck home when a man unknown to me in my parents' small town stopped me on the street and asked what it was like for me to know that my dad was living with another woman. Other verses from the laments were highlighted as I tried to reconcile my parents and bring them together, though with no success. "Plead my case, O Lord," I prayed, "fight my fight!" (see Ps 35:1).

Dad filed for divorce just a few days before their thirty-second wedding anniversary. I was in the middle of my

Hebrew qualifying exams. What made it worse was that I had five Masses to celebrate that weekend—two on Saturday and three on Sunday. The Gospel for all five liturgies was the prohibition of divorce in Mark 10:1-9. The Sunday, October 2, was my parents' wedding anniversary. The pain of having to preach against divorce on my parents' anniversary, just after they had filed for divorce, was almost unbearable. To avoid weeping openly I had to avoid looking at the people's faces in each congregation. What else could I do but pray the psalms of lament and feel the agony of each prayer that whole year?

St. Paul tells us to rejoice with those who rejoice and weep with those who weep (see Rom 12:15). I delight in the fact that the psalms, which are the source of the Church's official prayer, contain prayers that both rejoice and weep. I found myself in those laments, and it helped me to know that God is not distant from those who weep. The Christian life does not preclude grief and sadness but offers a place in which to bring these sufferings before God in profound biblical prayers. Instead of stifling my sadness, I could grow by voicing it before God in prayers whose structure helped me to express my feelings.

In addition, the same psalms of lament typically offer prayers of hope for final vindication from God (for example, see Ps 31:23-25). Their prayers of confidence offered me hope of eventual help from God, even though my efforts to help my family had been unsuccessful so far. How or when this help would come I did not know, but directed by the psalms I could pray for it with confidence.

The psalms of lament also opened my heart and mind to

another approach to suffering of different kinds: seeing the cross and resurrection of Jesus Christ as a pattern for the Christian life. Some of the torments of the Lord's passion are described in the laments, for example, the dividing of his garments and casting of lots for his outer cloak (see Ps 22:19) and being given vinegar to drink (see Ps 69:22). Our Lord Jesus prayed some of the laments while he was on the cross. "My God, my God, why have you forsaken me?" (Ps 22:1) "Father, into your hands I commend my spirit" (Ps 31:6).

Since Christ prayed these laments in the depths of his suffering, any Christian can turn to the same prayers in suffering. And since these psalms turn to prayers of confidence—as Christ's death results in resurrection—any Christian can expect the Lord to bring good out of tragedies and difficulties.

CRUCIFIED WITH CHRIST

Both the disciplinary experiences of suffering and the mysteriously painful ones form an essential aspect of being conformed to Christ. Certainly, the gospel does not present suffering as life's ultimate goal, but Jesus Christ does lay down norms for discipleship in terms of carrying one's cross. To his disciples and to the crowds, he insists that love of Christ must exceed love of family or self (see Mt 10:34-39; Lk 14:26-27). Aware of the pain this teaching would cause in his society, which was so focused on the family, Jesus adds, "Anyone who does not carry his own cross and come after me cannot be my disciple" (Lk 14:27).

Similarly, after St. Peter tries to dissuade Christ from talking about his coming suffering and death, Jesus says, "If anyone wishes to come after me, let him deny himself, pick up his cross and follow me. For whoever wishes to save his soul must lose it, and whoever loses his soul for my sake will find it" (Mt 16:24-25; see also Mk 8:34-37 and Lk 9:23-25).

St. Paul echoes the same doctrine in his epistles. Even when he proclaims the glorious power of the Holy Spirit to make us the adopted children of God, he includes the importance of suffering with Christ. We have become "heirs of God and co-heirs with Christ, as long as we suffer with him so as to be glorified with him" (Rom 8:15-17).

In the letter to the Galatians, St. Paul relates the message of the cross of Christ to his own experience of the world: "Let me not boast except in the cross of our Lord Jesus Christ, through which the world was crucified to me and I to the world" (Gal 6:14). Though the world is good— "every creature of God is good" (1 Tm 4:4)—being crucified to the world makes for a detachment which frees one from seeking ultimate fulfillment in this world. We humans need this crucifixion because we are typically tempted to cling to earthly things as ways to augment our ego and pride instead of using them for the greater glory of God. St. Paul develops this idea further in the letter to the Philippians:

But whatever gain I had, I counted as loss for the sake of Christ. Indeed I count everything as loss because of the surpassing worth of knowing Christ Jesus my Lord. For his sake I have suffered the loss of all things, and count them as refuse, in order that I may gain Christ and be found in him, not having a righteousness of my own, based on law, but that which is through faith in Christ, the righteousness from God that depends on faith; that I may know him and the power of his resurrection, and may share his sufferings, becoming like him in his death, that if possible I may attain the resurrection from the dead.

PHILIPPIANS 3:7-11

It is precisely his profound knowledge of Jesus Christ and his appreciation of the importance of God's righteousness which give St. Paul a proper perspective on the role of the good things of the world. By comparison, everything is passing rubbish, while knowledge of Christ and God's righteousness endure for all eternity. From that perspective, St. Paul—and every Christian—must be willing to share in Christ's suffering and conform to his death so as to share in his glorious resurrection from the dead.

"TAKE UP YOUR CROSS AND FOLLOW ME"

This is the perspective in which to see the great and small sufferings we experience in life, and specifically in our life in the Church. When we have exhausted our ideas for improving a frustrating situation and the problem persists, there is still something we can do. We can accept the pain, offer it up to the Lord in union with his suffering on the cross, and trust that he will bring about a greater victory than we had originally imagined.

No good whining about our pain, despairing over the future of the Church, and retreating in defeat. Faith does not collapse in the face of problems. Rather, faith in Christ Jesus involves a deeper and deeper living out of the paschal mystery that leads through death to new life.

Crosses large and small are inevitable in life; it is misguided to seek them out or try and find something more acceptable. Anyone who places his or her life in God's hands can be sure that their challenges and sufferings have been tailor-made for them. We can trust that God our Lord has important reasons for offering certain crosses rather than others.

Christians can also be certain that they do not carry their crosses alone. Jesus, who promised that his yoke would be easy and his burden light (see Mt 11:30), will always be present to carry the cross with us. Yokes are worn by a pair: each Christian is half the team, while Jesus Christ is the companion in pulling the burden. He carried the cross first and still leads every Christian who carries the cross.

"I am with you all days, until the end of the age," Jesus promised his disciples when he returned to the Father at the ascension (see Mt 28:20). This promise is for us, too. Especially when it seems that all the doors have closed and there is nothing left but to bide our time, how heartening to know that it is Jesus—the One who endured the cross in anticipation of the glory to come—who bears and sustains us as we wait.

NINE

Blessed Are the Frustrated

You might say that writing this book was an exercise in frustration.

For one thing, it took much longer than I had planned. Then a series of requests to have me assigned in Amman, Nairobi, Khartoum, Jerusalem, Rome, and finally Dallas kept my life in turmoil. Having my laptop computer stolen at Tel Aphek, Israel—the place where the Philistines took the Ark of the Covenant from the Israelites in the days of Samuel the prophet—did not help. Moving from Chicago to Dallas while teaching in San Diego did not make for ideal writing conditions either.

Throughout the whole process I have had ample opportunity to implement the approach to handling frustrations that I outlined in chapter one and described throughout the book. Naturally, I would gladly have foregone this opportunity in favor of some smoother sailing!

On the other hand, "it is enough for the disciple that he become like his teacher" (Mt 10:25). I want to be like

Jesus. And didn't Jesus encounter one frustration after another as he went about announcing the Good News of the kingdom of God? Just look at what the Gospels reveal on this point.

IN JESUS' FOOTSTEPS

Jesus' disciples are depicted as an obtuse bunch who never quite grasp his message until the day of Pentecost. They misunderstand Jesus, take his words too literally. "Do you not understand or comprehend? Are your hearts hardened?" Jesus asks them again and again. "Do you still not understand?" (Mk 8:17, 21). Peter confesses Jesus as the Messiah one moment but then turns around and opposes him the next. "Get behind me, Satan!" Jesus rebukes him. "You are an obstacle to me" (Mt 16:23). The disciples dishearten their Master by their petty quarrels over places of honor, their inability to keep watch for an hour—and, ultimately, their final desertion of Jesus.

The crowds around Jesus are fickle. On Palm Sunday they salute Jesus with palm branches and hosannas and welcome him into Jerusalem as their king; a few days later they crucify him on the other side of the city. Sometimes they follow Jesus because of his teaching, sometimes because they want bread (see Jn 6:26). Sometimes his teaching drives them away: "Do you also want to leave?" he asks the disciples after declaring himself the bread of life (see Jn 6:67). Jesus occasionally meets with faith, but more often he is "amazed" at the lack of it (see Mk 6:6). From time to time his exasperation erupts in exclamations like, "O faithless and perverse generation, how long will I be with you and endure you?" (Lk 9:41).

The religious leaders grieve and anger Jesus by their hardness of heart (see Mk 3:5). At every turn they oppose him, close their ears to him, seek to trip him up, even accuse him of being possessed (see Jn 8:48). How frustrating not to be able to overcome their lack of mercy, their hypocrisy, their preoccupation with the letter rather than the spirit of the law! Jesus miraculously fed a crowd of four thousand, and still the Pharisees demand "a sign from heaven to test him." No wonder Jesus sighed "from the depth of his spirit" (Mk 8:11-12)!

From the smallest frustrations to the greatest sorrows, Jesus experienced the whole range of challenges that life offers each one of us. He dealt with people who forgot his teachings (see Mt 16:5) and who didn't follow his directions (see Mk 1:44-45). He had to change his plans when things did not work out (see Lk 9:52-53). Crowds of needy people followed him around, making constant demands and creating inconvenient situations (see Mk 3:9). With great love Jesus gave everything he had, right down to his very life, and then watched as some people accepted and many rejected him.

So blessed indeed are those who are frustrated, for they follow in the footsteps of Jesus!

WHAT MAKES THE GOOD SOIL GOOD?

We the frustrated are also blessed because frustration is not the end of the story for those who cling to God. Jesus' greatest triumph, his resurrection from the dead, followed upon his greatest apparent failure, his suffering and death on the cross. This is the pattern for each individual Christian, too. Faithfulness to God in the midst of frustrations always reaps final rewards as well as benefits along the way, as God turns the experience to our profit.

What specific personal benefit can we expect as we try to tackle our frustrations in a godly way? Our Lord's parable of the sower and the seed gives one answer (see Mk 4:14-20).

Recall that in the parable, seed is scattered on four different types of soil. As Jesus explains to the disciples, the seed is the word of God, which receives different responses as it is announced. The pathway represents the people who have heard the word without accepting it. They symbolize hard, trampled down soil which is incapable of even admitting the seed; as the birds pick up the seed that has fallen on this hard ground, the devil quickly snatches the word from these closed hearts. The seed on thin soil grows up quickly, but it withers because the roots have no depth. Similarly, some people abandon the gospel at the first hint of challenge or opposition. The seed among the weeds takes root but is choked out, just as money and worldly cares choke out many people's focus on God's kingdom. Finally, the seed that falls on good ground, like Christians who persevere and bear fruit, yields an astounding harvest—thirty- or sixty- or a hundred-fold.

What makes the good soil in this parable so good? For one thing, soil must be plowed so that it is open to receive the seed. So too Christians need to have their lives plowed with suffering and reflection. Setbacks and frustrations are the time of plowing that give us depth. Reflection and meditation on the word of God and on our own suffering bring us wisdom.

The effect of this "plowing" is to open us to God's word so that it becomes firmly rooted in us, resonating within our whole being. It makes us humble when we succeed and confident of God's love when we fail. The depth of personality that comes through experiencing pain or suffering allows us to hear other people's pain and to respond with depth rather than in a superficial way. Also we become more authentic and credible witnesses to the Good News of Jesus Christ. When we ourselves have experienced that the gospel makes sense out of life's most difficult situations as well as its successes, we will announce it with the ring of truth that can catch the attention of other sufferers.

Every day brings opportunities to be good soil and to welcome the living word of God as it is sown in us. As we meditate on the gospel of Jesus and become familiar with both the Old and the New Testaments, as we apply it in our lives, we will become fruitful. Even when our efforts at correcting or addressing some frustrating situation meet with seeming failure, we will learn to live by hope in God's power to make the word bear fruit. After all, the growth of any seed takes time and is barely observable. And this is no ordinary seed but God's word, full of power and authority.

Vigorous seed and good soil add up to a bumper crop.

God's word and a heart made receptive by trials add up to a rich harvest of blessings—both for the frustrated Catholic and for the whole Church. The two stories that follow reveal something of this mysterious dynamic.

GOOD HARVEST IN THE GOLDEN YEARS

Ten years ago Tom and Jean were like any ordinary American couple planning for retirement. Grandchildren, golf, travel, senior citizen discounts—they looked forward to having more leisure time for these and other things. With the pension Tom had coming after his thirty years as a fireman, life would be comfortable.

Somewhere along the line, though, the seed of God's word began to germinate and take root in Tom and Jean, unsettling their tidy plans for the future. It happened through their discovery of the Bible. Mildly interested at first, they gradually became eager to learn all they could about God's word as they experienced its impact on their lives. They joined a Bible study group and attended talks and courses in local parishes. They signed up for a summer Scripture program at a Catholic university.

As their own interest in Scripture grew, Tom and Jean couldn't help but notice how few of their fellow Catholics they could share it with. "Why aren't Catholics more interested in the Bible?" they would wonder in frustration. "Why don't more priests encourage the study of Scripture?"

Fortunately Tom and Jean encountered one priest, a well-known Scripture scholar, who urged them to put their frustration to work by equipping themselves to make a difference for others. Encouraged by his support, the couple made a radical decision: Tom took an early retirement, they sold their house, took their money, and moved away to enroll in a Master's program in Scripture at a Catholic university. For the next few years Tom and Jean lived like typical graduate students instead of retirees—small apartment, small income, lots of studying.

Tom and Jean look back on that pivotal decision with no regrets. Today they work within a diocese, leading Bible study groups and training other Catholics to do the same. It is a shoestring operation and they live modestly, with little time or money for many of the recreations that occupy most people their age. But Tom and Jean are deeply motivated and grateful for the opportunity to help other Catholics discover the life-changing power of God's word—a message they preach not just by their words but by their very life.

"YOU DON'T TRUST GOD"

Roseanne was one of seven children—"too many for my parents to handle." As she saw it, her alcoholic mother and ineffectual father had abided by Catholic teaching on birth control only to end up with a large dysfunctional family and no help for raising them.

An illegitimate pregnancy when she was in her late teens only strengthened Roseanne's feeling that the Church should approve birth control. She wasn't sure about abortion but after struggling with the idea finally decided against it.

Once married, Roseanne felt no qualms about insisting on birth control, approved or not. The issue became a point of tension between her and her husband, who did not share her certainty on the matter. As this and other disagreements accumulated, their marriage began to falter.

It was when Roseanne realized that she was on a certain path to divorce that she began crying out to God. Oh, she had prayed before—but never with much feeling or persistence. But now that her life was threatening to unravel, Roseanne sought God in earnest. Through regular confession and the counsel of an experienced priest, she began to experience God's presence and guidance. Her marriage improved. Prompted by a friend's openness to a late-in-life pregnancy, she also began to rethink the issue of birth control.

That rethinking—along with reading, praying, and talking to other Catholics—led Roseanne to reverse her stand on birth control. Much of her frustration with the Church's teaching stemmed from fear, she now realized. "You don't trust God," her confessor had told her one day. He had been right. But now with her prayer life blossoming, Roseanne was discovering that God is loving and perfectly trustworthy. That did not remove all the uncertainties, but it did make it possible for Roseanne to finally place this part of her life fully in God's hands.

With Roseanne's new openness to life has come a new openness to serving God's people. Eager to use her experience to help others, she has found an outlet in the pro-life movement. Today Roseanne directs a counseling center that is helping many, many women to make pregnancy choices they will never regret.

WHAT ABOUT YOU?

What particular frustrations in your life as a Catholic are you facing at the moment? Are you struggling with some aspect of Church teaching that you do not understand, like Roseanne? Is there some weakness or lack in the Church that troubles you, as Tom and Jean were troubled? Or perhaps your frustration is totally different.

Whatever your situation, I encourage you to acknowledge it, with God's help, and to ask yourself the following questions.

What will happen if you take no action? Will this problem simply go away if it is ignored? Some problems do heal themselves over time, but serious infections only get worse. Does the pain caused by the problem outweigh the pain of working to correct it? What will happen—to you, to the Church, to the world—if you do nothing about this situation? What pain will be avoided? What benefits will be forfeited?

As I stated in chapter one, no book can offer solutions for the wide variety of frustrations that Catholics experience within the Church. But the approach suggested here is one that you can successfully adapt to fit the unique situations that frustrate you. The result could be your own and other people's spiritual renewal. Set goals, repent, pray, study, act, persevere: here is a strategy that can make a difference in your experience of life in the Church—and perhaps in other people's as well.

So truly blessed are we who are frustrated, for in our every frustration lies a choice opportunity to follow our Master, imitate him, and be transformed into his likeness. Not only that: in our struggles we can rely on the help of Jesus himself, "who has similarly been tested in every way, yet without sin" (Heb 4:15).

"And behold, I am with you always, until the end of the age" (Mt 28:20). This promise of Jesus—the last words recorded in Matthew's Gospel—must have carried the disciples through many a hard time. As we take it to heart in the midst of whatever frustrations we encounter, it will do the same for us.

NOTES

1. The issue of women's ordination has brought much pain to the American Church since the 1970s. Both liberals and conservatives from my own seminary agree that its closing was precipitated by rancor over this issue. Most ordinations were accompanied by meetings, weeping, anger, and rage. Once, in south Louisiana, some of the women students from the seminary protested by standing during the ordination ceremony and wearing blue arm bands to express how sad and blue they felt about their exclusion from ordination. At the end of Mass two Cajun ladies remarked, "Well, if I would have known that the Blue Army was going to be there, I would have worn my arm band, too!" The arm bands did not appear at later protests.

   The issue has not remained theoretical but has had great impact on the spiritual and liturgical lives of many. For instance, some women prefer not to attend Mass and instead create their own liturgies. They focus on their own experiences and on feminine images of God. Because women feel excluded from the liturgy, Sr. Donna Quinn, O.P., says, "We're not waiting for the boys anymore. We're getting too big for this church that seems to be dying. It can no longer contain our spirit." An anonymous nun who serves on her order's administrative team admitted that she rarely goes to Mass because it makes her so angry. She is "exhausted with and really offended by the constant referral to God as father, king, and lord. It's the arrogance of the whole thing," she said. However, she intends to remain within the Church because her pain causes her to create new ways of being church. (All quotes from Mary Beth Murphy, "Catholic Women Create Own Liturgy," *Milwaukee Sentinel,* November 16, 1992, 1A.)

   Another way in which this issue makes an impact is in the liturgical and educational life of the average parish through the related issue of gender inclusive language. Some Catholics hold that Jesus called God his Father simply because he was a product of a paternalistic society. For this reason, some lectionaries have pencil or ink marks to blot out every masculine pronoun referring to humanity or to God. The words Father, Son, Lord, and King may be removed. The congregation may be instructed to omit masculine pronouns in the Mass responses. Sometimes ordinary parts of Mass, like the Gloria or Creed, are omitted because of their use of "sexist" terms for God.

Other people are more radical and choose a completely different idea of God—either a neuter being or a masculine and feminine combination—in order to promote feminist empowerment and women's ordination. One feminist called the Trinity an "Old Boys Club." She prefers addressing God as the Creator, Redeemer, and Sanctifier. Others like to pray to God the Father/Mother, Son/Daughter, and Spirit. Sr. Lucy Edelbeck, O.P., of Milwaukee goes even further; she states that she has "come out of a Christian base, but for a long time, I've been drawn to develop woman spirituality in the Goddess tradition." For instance, she reclaims Mary, the Mother of Jesus, as a goddess rather than a passively sweet figure. (Lois Blinkhorn, "Women/In Search of Spirituality, In Search of Self," *Milwaukee Journal,* April 11, 1993, G6.)

2. Ann Roach Muggeridge, *The Desolate City: Revolution in the Catholic Church* (San Francisco: Harper and Row, 1986), 9-23.

3. For example, Sr. Sheila Lyne, a Catholic nun, holds a post as a city of Chicago health commissioner. Unfortunately, this Sister of Mercy publicly advocated governmental funding of abortions for the poor. She reasons that the poor deserve the same options for abortion as the middle class (as if there are not already enough killings among the poor in America.) After all, abortion is legal, she said in an interview on "At Issue," on WBBM-AM (April 17, 1994). Chicago's archbishop, Joseph Cardinal Bernardin, publicly rejected Sr. Sheila Lyne's position, but this nun continues to promote a goal of safe sex which completely ignores the Catholic goal of a safe eternal life.

4. Some liberal Catholics have organized themselves into groups which continue to oppose the official Church while remaining within it. Especially well known is Call To Action, an organization that sponsors a "We Are the Church" conference every autumn. Call To Action claims that 90 percent of its members attend Mass regularly, 63 percent are laity, 28 percent are women religious, and 9 percent are priests; one third, it says, are employed by the Church.

   Calling itself "a breath of air in a suffocating church," Call To Action seeks a "more inclusive, egalitarian, and grown-up" church that, as speaker Edwina Gately put it, worships a "warm, moist, salty God." Its ideology has been enunciated by other conference speakers like Mary Hunt, who said that it is wrong to call God "lord, ruler, and king" and have a "top-down hierarchical church," because both concepts cause violence in the modern world. (All quotes are from the *Call To Action News,* January 1995.)

5. Ignatius of Antioch, "To the Ephesians," 7, 2.

6. *Lumen Gentium,* "Dogmatic Constitution on the Church," par. 13.

7. *Lumen Gentium,* par. 15.

8. *Gaudium et Spes,* par. 45.

9. *Lumen Gentium*, par. 17.

10. *Gaudium et Spes*, par. 34.

11. Pope St. Gregory the Great, *The Moral Reflections on Job*, as quoted in *The Liturgy of the Hours* (New York: Catholic Book Publishing Company, 1975), 261-62.

12. *Our Sunday Visitor*, vol. 83, no. 41 (February 5, 1995), 5.

13. Fr. Benedict Groeschel, *The Reform of the Renewal* (San Francisco: Ignatius, 1990).

14. Council of Trent, "Decree on Original Sin," (1546) par. 5, quoted in *The Church Teaches* (Rockford, Ill.: TAN, 1973), 160.

15. *Catechism of the Catholic Church* (Libreria Editrice Vaticana, 1994), par. 1428.

16. *Lumen Gentium*, par. 8.

17. *Catechism*, par. 2631.

18. *Catechism*, par. 1430.

19. Fr. Joseph Champlin, *Together in Peace* (Notre Dame, Ind.: Ave Maria, 1974). Msgr. Louis Gaston de Segur, *Confession: A Little Book for the Reluctant* (Rockford, Ill.: TAN, 1989).

20. *Gaudium et Spes*, par. 4.

21. *Gaudium et Spes*, par. 17.

22. *Gaudium et Spes*, par. 26.

23. *Gaudium et Spes*, par. 27.

24. *Gaudium et Spes*, par. 28.

25. *Gaudium et Spes*, par. 29.

26. *Gaudium et Spes*, par. 47.

27. *Gaudium et Spes*, par. 49. See also the many Scripture passages that urge the nourishment of pure conjugal love and undivided affection: Genesis 2:22-23; Proverbs 5:15-20; 31:10-31; Tobit 8:4-8; Song of Songs 1:2-3, 16; 4:16; 5:1; 7:8-14; 1 Corinthians 7:3-6; Ephesians 5:25-33.

28. *Gaudium et Spes*, par. 48.

29. *Catechism*, par. 2599.

30. *Catechism*, par. 2602.

31. Christ's "seven last words" prayed from the cross: "My God, my God, why have you forsaken me?" (Mk 15:34; cf. Ps 22:2); "Father, into your hands I commit my spirit!" (Lk 23:46; Ps 31:6); "Father, forgive them, for they know not what they do" (Lk 23:34); "Truly, I say to you, today you will be with me in Paradise" (Lk 23:43); "Woman, behold your son. Son, Behold your Mother" (Jn 19:26-27); "I thirst" (Jn 19:28); "It is finished" (Jn 19:30).

32. *Catechism*, par. 2560, referring to St. Augustine, "De diversis quaestionibus octoginta tribus" 64, 4 (Patrologia Latina: 40, 56).

33. *Catechism*, par. 2558, referring to St. Thérèse of Lisieux, *Manuscrits autobiographiques*, C 25r.

34. *Catechism,* pars. 2562, 2563.

35. *Catechism,* par. 2565.

36. See also Phil 2:6-11; Col 1:15-20; Eph 5:14; 1 Tm 3:16; 6:15-16; 2 Tm 2:11-13—all composed under the inspiration of the Holy Spirit and reflecting the mystery of God's salvation in Christ.

37. *Catechism,* par. 2650; see also *Dei Verbum,* "Dogmatic Constitution on Divine Revelation," par. 8.

38. *Catechism,* par. 2653, quoting *Dei Verbum,* par 25, and referring to Phil 3:8 and St. Ambrose, "De officiis ministrorum," 1, 20, 88 (Patrologia Latina: 16, 50).

39. *Catechism,* par. 2723.

40. *Catechism,* par. 2715, referring to St. Ignatius of Loyola, *Spiritual Exercises,* 104.

41. *Catechism,* pars. 1174-78. On prayer see also pars. 2587-2589, 2691, 2698, 2700.

42. *Catechism,* pars. 2670-71.

43. This tradition is developed in a marvelous reflection on the Hail Mary, the rosary, and other Marian prayers in the *Catechism,* pars. 2675-79.

44. *Catechism,* par. 2683.

45. *Catechism,* par. 2684.

46. Some good modern books on prayer include *The Practice of the Presence of God,* by Brother Lawrence (Springdale, Penn: Whitaker House, 1982); *The Art of Praying,* by Monsignor Romano Guardini, and *Spiritual Passages,* by Fr. Benedict Groeschel (New York: Crossroad Publishing, 1983).

47. *Catechism,* par. 2689.

48. *Catechism,* par. 2691.

49. For more information about Fr. Martin Lucia's work, contact Mrs. Katie Pfeffer (713) 468-7279.

50. *Catechism,* par. 2685.

51. *Catechism,* par. 2691.

52. To receive a copy of Lenny Alt's newsletter or to discuss strategies, write Lenny Alt, P.O. Box 1356, Milwaukee, WI 53201-1356.

53. St. Mary's University in San Antonio, Texas, holds a summer Bible seminar each year. (One Camino Santa Maria, San Antonio, Texas; 210-436-3126.) Franciscan University of Steubenville, in Ohio, holds various summer conferences directed to different age groups. The University also has a Distance Education department that enables Catholics anywhere to take for-credit graduate and undergraduate courses in theology, philosophy, and history. (Franciscan University of Steubenville, Steubenville, Ohio, 43952-6701; 614-283-6226.) The University of Dallas runs the Institute for Religious and Pastoral Studies, which offers a masters' degree to Catholics in certain dioceses (as of this writing, San Diego, California;

Portland, Oregon; and Fargo, North Dakota). Presentation Ministries in Cincinnati, Ohio, offers summer workshops in Scripture.

This by no means exhausts the list of sources for sound Catholic teaching of the Bible. Look around to find the ones that fit your needs, and then learn as much as time and resources allow.

54. *The Companion to the Catechism of the Catholic Church* (San Francisco: Ignatius).

55. Vatican II itself is a gift of the Holy Spirit to the Church, but quite often the supposed "spirit of Vatican II" is invoked incorrectly. The Council taught no new doctrines but reaffirmed the teachings of the Church. Contrary to the claims made by some, the Vatican Council did not take away belief in purgatory, confession, or the role of the pope as the Vicar of Christ on earth. No document teaches that all religions are equally good paths to reach the same God, yet the documents do teach a proper ecumenism and respect for the truth present in other religions. Vatican II calls the laity to exercise their apostolate as mature Christians, while at the same time confirming that the priests act *in persona Christi* (in the person of Christ) when they celebrate the sacraments.

56. *The Documents of Vatican II,* ed. Austin Flannery, O.P. (Grand Rapids, Mich.: Eerdmans Publishing, 1975). See also *The Documents of Vatican II: More Postconciliar Documents,* ed. Austin Flannery, O.P. (Grand Rapids, Mich.: Eerdmans Publishing, 1983).

57. John Hardon, S.J. is known for his popular catechetical works including his study guide to *The Catechism of the Catholic Church,* entitled *The Faith* (Ann Arbor, Mich.: Servant, 1995). Some of his previous works include *The Catholic Catechism* (New York: Doubleday, 1979), *The Question and Answer Catholic Cathechism* (New York: Doubleday, 1981), and *The Pocket Catholic Catechism* (New York: Doubleday, 1989).

58. Kenneth Baker, S.J., *The Fundamentals of Catholicism* (San Francisco: Ignatius, 1983).

59. Ludwig Ott, *Fundamentals of Catholic Dogma* (Rockford, Ill.: Tan Books, 1974). Readers can look these up in Denzinger-Schoenmetzer, *Enchiridion Symbolorum* or in *The Church Teaches: Documents of the Church in English Translation* (Rockford, Ill.: Tan Books).

60. Eberhardt's, *A Summary of Catholic History* is now out of print. Warren H. Carroll, *The Building of Christendom* (Front Royal, VA: Christendom Press, 1987).

61. Keep in mind that not all of the facts presented by certain Protestant apologists are true. For example, Lorraine Boettner claims that the medieval Catholic Church placed the Bible on the Index of Forbidden Books at the Council of Valencia in A.D. 1229—even though there were no councils in Valencia, and the Index was not established until A.D. 1543 (Cited in Karl Keating, *Catholicism and Fundamentalism,* 44-45; see note 84.)

62. William Jurgens, *The Faith of the Early Fathers* (Collegeville, Minn.: Liturgical Press, 1979). Johannes Quasten, *Patrology* (Westminster, MD: Christian Classics, 1983).

63. C.S. Lewis, *Mere Christianity* (New York: Macmillan Publishing, 1986). *Miracles: A Preliminary Report* (New York: Macmillan Publishing, 1978). *The Problem of Pain* (New York: Macmillan Publishing, 1978). *The Weight of Glory* (New York: Macmillan Publishing, 1980). *God in the Dock* (Grand Rapids, Mich.: Eerdmans Publishing, 1972). *The Abolition of Man* (New York: Macmillan Publishing, 1978).

   And don't overlook C.S. Lewis the novelist. His *Chronicles of Narnia* (New York: Macmillan Publishing, 1986) exemplify the rich use of the Christian imagination. (They are not only for children, by the way: I have read them multiple times and love them!) His space trilogy—*Out of the Silent Planet, Perelandra,* and *That Hideous Strength* (New York: Macmillan, 1987)—demonstrates how effctive sci-fi can be when it draws from Christian rather than New Age themes.

64. G.K. Chesterton, *The Everlasting Man (Ashville, N.C.: Revival Literature), Orthodoxy* (New York: Doubleday), *Heretics, The Catholic Church and Conversion* (San Francisco: Ignatius Press, 1990).

65. Frank Sheed, *Theology for Beginners* (Ann Arbor, Mich.: Servant, 1982). *Theology and Sanity* (San Francisco: Ignatius Press, 1994).

66. *This Rock. The Catholic Answer. Hands On Apologetics. Catholic Dossier. Crisis. First Things. New Covenant. Our Sunday Visitor. National Catholic Register. Catholic World Report.*

67. For instance, the League has taken action when federal and state funds are used to finance art exhibits mocking Christ or the Blessed Virgin Mary. On January 20, 1994, Dr. William Donahue, who now directs the League, published an open letter to President Clinton asking him to "vigorously denounce attacks against the Catholic Church." Former Surgeon General Joycelyn Elders and Faith Mitchell of the State Department both made anti-Catholic remarks, and the League worked to have them stopped.

   For help or for information on starting a chapter of the Catholic League for Religious and Civil Rights or supporting its work, contact: Catholic League, 1011 First Ave., New York, NY, 10022; (212) 371-3191, fax (212) 371-3394.

68. Scott Butler's research on Peter's confession of faith (Mt 16:18) and papal infallibility has led him and two friends to write a book on the subject. He phoned a well-known Patristics scholar to ask why no one has written more fully on the topic of the meaning of this text. The answer was that ecumenical concerns led scholars to move away from trying to prove papal infallibility. Since Scott knew so many ministers for whom papal infallibility

is still a hot issue, he read over two hundred books on the papacy and examined the councils and the Fathers of the Church for their testimony. The result is a book that does what the scholars had not done. Scott and his friends are publishing it privately in order to keep down the costs, avoid high prices, and finance sending copies to at least forty thousand Protestant ministers and professors.

69. *The Liturgy Documents* (Archdiocese of Chicago: Liturgy Training Publications). Pope John Paul II, *Inaestimabile Donum.*

70. *Sacrosanctum Concilium,* "Constitution on the Sacred Liturgy," par. 1.

71. *Sacrosanctum Concilium,* par. 21.

72. *Sacrosanctum Concilium,* par. 22.

73. *Sacrosanctum Concilium,* par. 23.

74. *Sacrosanctum Concilium,* par. 36.

75. *Sacrosanctum Concilium,* par. 37.

76. Such ceremonies have been used in Catholic churches and are encouraged by Starhawk, the self-proclaimed witch on the staff of Matthew Fox's Institute in Culture and Creation Spirituality.

77. For more information, write to: CREDO, c/o Fr. Cornelius O'Brien, P.O. Box 7004, Arlington, VA, 22207.

78. *Adoremus Bulletin,* vol. 1, no. 1, (November 1995), 2. For subscription and other information contact: Adoremus, P. O. Box 5858, Arlington, VA, 22205; (703) 241-5858.

79. Among other publications which make known the Church's official legislation on the liturgy are *Laywitness,* a publication of Catholics United for the Faith, and *Christifidelis,* a publication of the St. Joseph Foundation.

A related publication of a somewhat different type is *The Latin Mass Magazine,* which aims to inform and educate Catholics about their Latin and Gregorian chant heritage and encourage its development along the norms set out by Vatican II. Anyone interested in this quarterly publication can write to: *The Latin Mass Magazine,* 1331 Red Cedar Circle, Ft. Collins, CO, 80524.

80. *Sacrosanctum Concilium,* par. 34.

81. Some of them, like Tim Staples, have become active Catholic apologists, influencing many other people to become Catholic.

Tim tells his story in a book by Patrick Madrid, called *Surprised by Truth: 11 Converts Give the Biblical and Historical Reasons for Becoming Catholic* (San Diego, Calif.: Basilica Press, 1994).

82. Karl Keating, *Catholicism and Fundamentalism* (San Francisco: Ignatius, 1988) and *What Catholics Really Believe: 52 Answers to Common Misconceptions about the Catholic Faith* (Ann Arbor, Mich.: Servant, 1992).

83. Anyone who would like copies of tapes of the Catholic Answers debates, talks, or books, or would like to order *This Rock* magazine, contact the

organization at: Catholic Answers, P.O. Box 17490, San Diego, CA, 91977; (619) 541-1131, fax (619) 541-1154.

84. Information on the St. Joseph Foundation is based on the lead article in *Christifidelis*, vol. 12, no. 5 (October 15, 1994), 1, 7-8, as well as on a telephone interview with Charles Wilson.

   To request information about the St. Joseph Foundation newsletter, *Christifidelis*, or to help subsidize its work (the Foundation wishes to serve rich and poor alike and therefore does not charge for its services), contact: The Saint Joseph Foundation, 11107 Wurzbach, #404, San Antonio, TX, 78230-2553; (210) 697-0717. Or contact The St. Joseph Canonical Foundation of Canada (La Fondation Canonique St. Joseph du Canada), P.O. Box 9274, Ottawa, Canada K1G3T9, Ralph W. Stewart, Executive Director.

85. See *Lumen Gentium*, par. 28, and *Presbyterorum Ordinis*, Decree on the Ministry and Life of Priests, par. 2.

86. *In Persona Christi*, PO Box 13725, Portland, OR, 97213.

87. For more information about the magazine or books, contact: *The Catholic Answer*, 200 Noel Plaza, Huntington, IN, 46750; (800) 348-2440.

88. To find out about getting broadcasts in your area, call the marketing department of EWTN at (205)956-9537.

89. Pope John Paul II's encyclical, *Christifidelis Laici* ("The Lay Members of Christ's Faithful People"), promoted the acceptance of lay associations, with canonical legislation to govern and protect an association's members. This canonical structure and status, which gives associations a name and place in official church life, facilitates communication with bishops and other leaders around the world. See *Christifidelis Laici*, Vatican Translation (Boston, Mass.: St. Paul Books and Media, December 30, 1988).

90. Here, the important criticisms of Thomas Day are most useful for summoning Catholics back to beauty. See his books, *Why Catholics Can't Sing* (New York: Crossroad Publishing, 1990), and *Where Have You Gone, Michelangelo?* (New York: Crossroad Publishing, 1993).

91. David Wilkerson, *The Cross and the Switchblade* (Grand Rapids, Mich.: Baker Book House, 1981).